A TRIBUTE TO
HEATH LEDGER
THE ILLUSTRATED BIOGRAPHY

A TRIBUTE TO
HEATH LEDGER
THE ILLUSTRATED BIOGRAPHY

Chris Roberts

CARLTON
BOOKS

THIS IS A CARLTON BOOK

First published by
Carlton Books Limited 2008
20 Mortimer Street
London W1T 3JW

ISBN 978-1-84732-169-5

Editorial Manager: Rod Green
Art Director: Lucy Coley
Designer: Anna Pow
Picture Research: Steve Behan
Production: Claire Hayward

Printed in Dubai

CHRIS ROBERTS has written about film and music for a wide range of international publications and websites including *Elvis*, *Uncut*, *The Guardian*, *London Lite* and Channel 4.com. As a broadcaster he appears on BBC, Sky News and others. His previous books include *Scarlett Johansson*, *Lou Reed*, *Abba* and *Idle Worship*.

PICTURE CREDITS

The publishers would like to thank the following sources for their kind permission to reproduce the pictures in this book.

Big Picturesphoto.com: GIG110 left.

Rex Features: 4, 17 left, 55 left, 69; /Dave Allocca 109; /Matt Baron/BEI 8, 79, 104; /Mel Bouzad 53; /Stephen Butler 16, 61 left; /Humberto Carreno 10 left, 102 left, 103; /Peter Carrette 17 right, 43 right, 61 right; /Charbonneau/BEI 65; /Carolyn Contino/BEI 83; /Steve Connolly 89; /Stewart Cook 12, 44 left & right; /Carlos Costas 88 right; /Marion Curtis 19, 78; /Bill Davila 80; /Everett Collection 2, 9, 24, 30, 31, 32, 34, 35, 36, 37, 40, 42, 45, 46, 47, 48, 50, 54, 56, 57, 58, 59, 64 left & right, 66 top & bottom, 67, 70, 71, 74 top & bottom, 75, 76, 77, 90, 92, 93, 94, 95, 96, 97 left, 97 right, 100, 101 left, 110 right, 111; / Jonathan Hayward 11; /David Heerde 98; /Icon Images: 60 right; /Munawar Hosain 22; /KPA/Zuma 102 right; /Paul Lovelace 106 left; /Jen Lowery 106 right; /Gabriella Mero 6; /Camilla Morandi 81; /Newspix 10 right, 14, 15, 20, 23, 25, 26, 28, 60 left, 73, 88 left, 107; /NBCU Photobank 112; /Alex Oliviera 38 right, 39 left; /Tess Peni 18, 38 left; / Romaniello/Venturelli 101 right; / David Silpa 84; /Sipa Press 87; /Jim Smeal 82; /BEI; /Snap 27; /Dan Steinberg/BEI 68; /Richard Young 39 right, 43 left, 55 right.

The Kobal Collection: 51, 52, 62, 86.

Newspix: 33.

Every effort has been made to acknowledge correctly and contact the source and/or copyright holder of each picture and Carlton Books Limited apologizes for any unintentional errors or omissions, which will be corrected in future editions of this book.

Contents

Introduction

WHEN THE CAST OF *Batman: The Dark Knight* was first
officially announced, the director, Christopher Nolan,
was asked, 'Why Heath Ledger as The Joker?'
Nolan's reply was succinct: 'Because he's fearless.'
Heath Ledger was born on 4 April 1979 and died, aged just
twenty-eight, on 22 January 2008. The gifted Australian
actor was found unconscious in his New York apartment.
An initial autopsy proved inconclusive but soon a coroner's
report announced that Ledger died of an accidental
overdose of prescription drugs. Warner Brothers, the
studio behind the *Batman* film which was set to make him
one the world's biggest screen icons, issued the
following statement:
'We are stunned and devastated by this tragic news. The
entertainment community has lost an enormous talent.
Heath was a brilliant actor and an exceptional person.
Our hearts go out to his family and friends.'

LEFT: Heath clowning for a photo
shoot with an image of himself
taped to the crate

LEFT: Heath with Michelle Williams at the Independent Spirit Awards in Los Angeles in 2007

ABOVE: Heath playng one of the 'Bob Dylan' characters in Todd Haynes' movie *I'm Not There*

Actress Michelle Williams, Ledger's former fiancée and mother of his two-year-old daughter, Matilda, released – on 1 February – her own personal statement to the media:

'Please respect our need to grieve privately. My heart is broken. I am the mother of the most tender-hearted, high-spirited, beautiful little girl, who is the spitting image of her father. All I can cling to is his presence inside her that reveals itself every day. His family and I watch Matilda as she whispers to trees, hugs animals and takes two steps at a time, and we know that he is with us still. She will be brought up with the best memories of him.'

Cinema fans will keep their own memories of the young man who, after his initial breakthrough with the enjoyable romantic comedy *Ten Things I Hate About You* bravely refused – as had Johnny Depp before him – to be typecast as the generic hunk, the vacuously handsome heart-throb. Holding out for more challenging roles, he had a few hit-and-miss years, with roles in films as varied as *The Patriot*, *A Knight's Tale*, *Monster's Ball* and *The Brothers Grimm*, before being Oscar-nominated for his impressively quiet yet resonant showing, opposite Jake Gyllenhaal (godfather to his child), as the inwardly tormented Ennis Del Mar in Ang Lee's subversive Western, *Brokeback Mountain*.

He continued to display his versatility through movies like Lasse Hallstrom's *Casanova* and the cultish *Candy*. Before his untimely death he'd last been seen in Todd Haynes' fascinating *I'm Not There*, playing one of six 'incarnations' of Bob Dylan, alongside his compatriot Cate Blanchett, Christian Bale (his Batman adversary), and Richard Gere. He was halfway through filming Terry Gilliam's

ABOVE: Skateboarding remained a passion for Heath throughout his life

ABOVE: Although he would grow to detest the 'heart-throb' label, Heath was not above striking a sultry pose

RIGHT: Quiet moments were rare for Heath who said his mind was constantly racing

The Imaginarium of Doctor Parnassus when tragedy struck. It's very possible that, as his last completed role, his wild interpretation of The Joker, a cross between Sid Vicious and Alex from *A Clockwork Orange*, will prove to be the part for which posterity best remembers him. The film will, undoubtedly, be massive. Yet his subtle, heart-wrenching performance in *Brokeback Mountain* could endure as one of cinema's most telling and influential. His death means so much promise and potential will remain untapped. 'I don't have a day planner or a diary,' he once said. 'I completely live in the now, not in the past, not in the future.'

The coroner's report said the cause of Heath Ledger's death was 'acute intoxication caused by the combined effects' of a group of anti-anxiety medications, painkillers and sleeping aids. 'We have concluded,' it went on, 'that the manner of death is accident, resulting from the abuse of prescription medications.' For weeks, Ledger had been complaining of being unable to sleep, his mind racing. The hope is that his legacy lives on in the energetic and

thoughtful acting performances committed to celluloid. Heath Ledger, born in Perth, had always been hungry to learn, had always strived for something more. His brief life and sometimes brilliant work merit both investigation and celebration.

In the course of this book we'll look at his upbringing (born to a well-off family), his youthful prowess in everything from art and dancing to sport; his ambition; his travels across Australia and then, via Hollywood, across the world. We will look at the early TV parts (including the inevitable rite-of-passage stint in Aussie TV soap *Home and Away*) and small movie roles, some valuable, some undistinguished. We will look at the first films which brought him a level of recognition and popularity. We will look at his insistence on expanding his repertoire as an actor beyond 'pin-up'. We will look at that towering and controversial *Brokeback Mountain* performance which deservedly won him the admiration of his peers and of global audiences. We will also look at his jaw-dropping Joker, surely the outstanding

blockbuster movie villain of 2008.

As well as this there are the romances to explore. During the course of his twenties, Ledger, who had admitted to a penchant for older women, dated such luminaries as Heather Graham, Naomi Watts and model Christina Cauchi. While he remained very close to Michelle Williams (whom he had met on the set of *Brokeback Mountain*) at the time of his death, he was reported to be seeing Mary-Kate Olsen. The media reaction to his demise was, in itself, a compelling and strange international phenomenon.

While it remains important to retain some sense of proportion and perspective, the current explosion of interest around Heath Ledger is unlikely to be revealed as mere hot-headed sentimentality. It is possible – probable, even – that the highlights among his body of work will earn him the kind of canonization granted, in earlier generations, to James Dean or River Phoenix. And while it seems he was deeply troubled at the time of his death, he'd told *Vanity Fair* in 2000, just as his star began to rise rapidly, that, 'I only do

this because I'm having fun. The day I stop having fun, I'll just walk away. There's so much I want to discover.'

Let's discover what we can about the man who once said, 'I like to do something I fear. I like to set up obstacles and defeat them. I like to be afraid of the project. I always am. When I get cast in something, I always believe I shouldn't have been. I fooled them again. I can't do it. I don't know how to do it. There's a huge amount of anxiety that drowns out any excitement I have toward the project.' The actor described by Christopher Nolan as 'fearless' was evidently, like all artists who capture the imagination, a web of contradictions. Which may be what drew him to characters like Robbie in *I'm Not There*, like Ennis in *Brokeback Mountain*, even like *Casanova* or *Ned Kelly*. Even, with that clash between darkness and hysteria, The Joker. As the poet John Normanton wrote in his meditation on late movie legends, 'Stars in an Oldie':

'Still, something's recorded of them. Though it may not comfort any who loved them . . . these are the stars . . .'

CHAPTER ONE

Raw Material

HEATH LEDGER – NAMED AFTER the hero of *Wuthering Heights*, Heathcliffe – was born Heath Andrew Ledger on 4 April, 1979, at the Subiaco Hospital in Perth, Western Australia. In Perth, the Ledger family were well-known and well-off. Their forefathers had run the foundry – The Ledger Engineering Foundry – which supplied raw material for the important Perth to Kalgoorlie pipeline, completed in 1903. Running 557 kilometres east into the desert, this pipeline pumped water to the Western Australia goldfields, serving over a hundred thousand people – not to mention six million sheep – across 44,000 square miles. Named after Heath's great grandfather (the son of Edson Ledger), the Sir Frank Ledger Charitable Trust was much respected for granting funds to the universities of the area, thus sponsoring scholarships for talented students and paying the fees of visiting lecturers.

LEFT: Heath attending the *Lords of Dogtown* premiere in Los Angeles in 2005

ABOVE: An informal pose from a
sun tanned young Ledger in 1999

RIGHT: A promising athlete, Heath gave
up his sporting career in favour of acting

Of Scottish and Irish descent, Heath grew up in an affluent household which enjoyed a healthy female influence (despite his father Kim's passion for car racing and ability to run several engineering firms simultaneously). Mother Sally was Sally Ramshaw, daughter of John and Jackie, and a descendant of the Scottish Campbell clan. A French teacher, she was a true romantic who named her first daughter Catherine after falling in love with Emily Brontë's classic novel *Wuthering Heights*. Catherine, now married to Nathan Buckey, prefers to be called Kate. Four years later, Heath, named after Heathcliffe, arrived. Heath's parents split when he was ten and two more half-sisters followed: Olivia Ledger and Ashleigh Bell. His stepfather was Roger Bell, his stepmother Emma Brown.

Heath was to tell *Cosmopolitan* in 1998 that, growing up in his teens with his mother and sisters, 'I learned respect for women, and patience. You grow up with all those women around you . . . you learn to wait your turn.'

There's a tale, perhaps apocryphal, that he sneaked a 'pet' kangaroo home at a young age, only for his mother to find it and liberate it. So close remained the family bonds years later that, weeks after Heath's daughter Matilda was

born, his mother and Kate flew from Australia to look after the baby while Heath and Michelle Williams undertook promotional duties for *Brokeback Mountain*.

As he grew up, however, he was still very much involved with his speed-freak father, who clearly impressed upon his boy the significance of a competitive spirit. Heath's early school days involved an enjoyable all-round education in sports. Guildford Grammar School was an all-boy private boarding academy, fifteen kilometres to the north east of Perth, benefiting from a hundred hectares of scenic land beside the Swan river. It boasted a dedication to 'the growth and freedom of young minds and bodies.' And a farm.

Little surprise, then, that Heath was content to be educated here for ten years. His relaxation options included full use of the playing fields, horse riding, or rowing on the river. There was an Olympic-size swimming pool. If he felt like singing, he could join the school choir in one of the most inspiring examples of Gothic architecture in the whole of the Australian continent – the Chapel of St Mary and St George.

Chiefly attended by the sons of wealthy farmers, the school also maintained a military tradition. Cadets were

LEFT: Heath at Flemington Racecourse in Melbourne with girlfriend Christina Cauchi in 2001

RIGHT: Heath's globetrotting lifestyle also saw him in London in 2001

FAR RIGHT: Posing for photographers in Sydney while promoting *A Knight's Tale* in 2001

trained in the use of firearms. Heath, already considered by some of his classmates to have maverick tendencies, elected to avoid this particular aspect of school life.

Instead, he threw himself into sport, excelling at cricket, Australian Rules football and especially field hockey, in which he became one of the youngest ever players to be selected for the school's first team. By 1990 he'd become a vital member of the Kalamunda field hockey team, and not just because his father, Kim, was president from 1990–92. His talent was to be confirmed later when he was selected for the State Under-Seventeen squad, and tipped as an up-and-coming star. He chose then, however, to drop the sport and pursue a career in acting.

When not at school, Heath maintained an active lifestyle by surfing, skateboarding and fishing: almost obligatory activities for any healthy young man in the Perth area. As a bonding exercise with his father, he hung out in the pits of motor sport and speedway events (happy to watch his father race), and himself won a few contests as a go-kart racer.

But it wasn't just running and leaping which appealed to the young Ledger. He showed an early interest in unconventional art, decorating his room with abstract paintings. He was a quick learner with enthusiasm and curiosity to burn.

Then, crucially, came the whetting of his appetite for the dramatic arts. His sister Kate had led the way. She'd

appeared on stage at the Globe Theatre with Perth's Shakespearean company: Heath, watching her, and already taking drama lessons, caught the bug. Given the choice at school between learning cooking or drama, he didn't hesitate to opt for the latter. By the age of ten he was treading the boards himself, taking the lead role in the Globe's production of *Peter Pan*.

Despite its success, several teachers attempted to dissuade the boy from pursuing his interest further, but this only fired his passion. From age twelve he workshopped plays with The Globe Shakespeare Company and the Midnight Youth Acting Company. He loved movies old and new: he was magnetised by his first screen idol, Gene

Kelly, of *Singing in the Rain* fame.

Again learning with dazzling speed, Heath taught himself to dance in the style of Kelly, and set about organising a Guildford Grammar dance team. Overcoming his schoolmates' resistance to an activity that wasn't at that time and in that place perceived as sufficiently macho, as well as the stark fact that most of them couldn't dance a step when he began disciplining them, he led a sixty-strong troupe to the first ever all-male victory at a national competition, the Rock Eisteddfod. Almost perversely, his self-devised routine was based on the theme of fashion. It was an early indication that when he set his determined mind and agile body to something, this boy could make things happen

ABOVE: Heath handling a press conference in 2000 rather well for someone who said he never had any clear plan about 'getting into the movie industry'

RIGHT: Heath with Matt Damon at the *Syriana* post-premiere party in New York in 2005

against all odds, peer pressures and prevailing trends.

His parents' split in 1989 prompted Heath to throw himself with even renewed vigour into these various productive activities. Meanwhile, sister Kate's agent had signed him up and sought to find him acting work. He was becoming increasingly fascinated by drama, to the detriment of his sporting pastimes. This led to him being 'leaned on' to make a choice between the two. He was, perhaps,the kind of good-at-everything child who unwittingly makes other children jealous. He had no clear plan about 'getting into the movie industry', but had enough youthful energy to juggle with his options and consider all of the possibilities.

In an interview years later he was to declare, rather strangely, 'I never studied acting in Australia.'

He added, even more cryptically, 'I never had an empty stage and black pyjamas in which to run around and express myself.'

Whatever the selective memory involved in that wilfully contrary statement, his first job as an extra was to come in 1992, when he was just thirteen. This fleeting debut occurred in a locally-produced TV series called *Clowning Around*, which starred Ernie Dingo. The storyline revolved around the adventures of a boy who runs away to join the circus.

Heath Ledger may not have been about to do something as obviously symbolic as that, exactly, but the art of acting was now to course through his veins for the rest of his brief, bright-burning life.

175cm

170cm

160cm

HEATH
LEDGER

DATE 14·07·95

CHAPTER TWO

The Roaring Boy

Heath – known to pals as 'Heathy' – was up and running. It would be too much to suggest that by beginning with *Clowning Around* and climaxing with The Joker we can discern a certain wry symmetry to his career, rather the fact that he was now committed to acting is key. His sister's influence had been important, and of all the paths open to him this is the one he wholeheartedly chose.

Field hockey, at least, had to take a back seat.

In 1993, the fourteen-year-old Ledger appeared in Australian TV show *Ship to Shore*, filmed, like *Clowning Around*, in Perth. This has been described as 'an Australian *Happy Days*', with good-looking teens goofing around, enjoying friendships and flirtations. There were also brief appearances in *Bush Patrol* and *Corrigan*.

LEFT: An early casting mugshot of Heath aged sixteen

Heath still had some growing up and studying to do, but by the time of his next role, in 1995, he was sixteen and within sight of young manhood. Also shot in Perth, the series *Sweat*, a definite progression from previous, test-the-waters parts, utilised his sporting competence. *Sweat* rotated around the lives of a bunch of teenagers and their ups and downs at an elite sports academy, something to which Heath could easily relate.

And it's here that we can really begin to trace the intelligence, ambition and bold spirit which distinguished Ledger from a thousand other wannabes. He was offered the choice between two parts, a swimmer or a cyclist. As the cyclist, Steve 'Snowy' Bowles, was a gay character, he plumped for that. Gay characters were an extreme rarity on Australian television at the time, and Heath loved taking risks. Also, he figured that taking the role would inevitably garner him attention. He'd stand out from the pack; he might even be more likely to be 'discovered'. Certainly such roles, however unmemorable in themselves, must have helped Ledger as training exercises. We can see why he would not have hesitated for a moment when offered the legendary *Brokeback Mountain* role years later, however many advisors may have told him that, now he was a 'name', it could jeopardise his career and bank-ability.

The show lasted twenty-six episodes and, although it was no artistic triumph (the general standard of acing was deemed to be poor), Heath was indeed spotted. He caught the attention not only of the casting scouts, but also of another member of the cast, one Martin Henderson, who was playing the part of Tom Nash. Henderson, then aged twenty, recognised instantly that Ledger had something

LEFT: When Heath arrived in Sydney to start his new life he had just sixty-nine cents in his pocket

ABOVE: Ledger, seated wearing red vest, with the cast of the Australian TV show *Sweat*, in which he played a gay cyclist

extra that the average young aspiring actor did not. He was four years older than Ledger, but the pair became great friends. Henderson has since achieved a high level of film and theatre success, starring in, among others, the movie *The Ring* (with Ledger's later lover, Naomi Watts).

So tight was the friendship that when Henderson went home to Sydney after the demise of *Sweat*, he phoned Ledger and urged him to pack his bags, come to the bigger city and take his chances in Australian acting's big league. Ledger was naturally hesitant at first: his family, friends and everything he knew centred around Perth. But his drive won the day.

Still only sixteen, he turned up at Henderson's Sydney apartment with minimal baggage and – remaining a sports enthusiast at heart – his beloved surfboard. He crashed in his new friend's living room and entered an exciting new phase in his life, rich with novel experiences, learning, culture and fun. When not surfing, he hung out with Henderson and was introduced to new people, sophisticated in the milieu of movies and TV.

Loving what he saw, and now showing the fearlessness that would come to characterise his life, he returned to Perth intent on leaving school. He discussed his decision with his mother, then gathered together his belongings. He also talked with his best buddy, Trevor DiCarlo, whom he had known since he was three years old. Enthused by Heath's belief that Sydney would be the place where their dreams all came true, DiCarlo decided to come along, too. Like so many young people before and since, they thought the city streets would be paved with, if not gold, at least connections. Nothing, it seemed, could dampen their enthusiasm or

dent their optimism. The pair drove over three thousand kilometres to Sydney and moved into Henderson's place.

Ledger later claimed to have had just sixty-nine cents in his pocket at that time. Soon, the trio moved into an apartment in Bondi, handily located for surfing. Ledger began to repay Henderson's kindness by teaching him to surf. They would wake up before sunrise to surf the waves on the northern beaches of Bondi. Of course, it wasn't all healthy sports and discussions on the thespian arts: the three young men weren't so earnest that they couldn't enjoy their fair share of hedonistic parties, drinking and girls. Ledger was loyal, too: Di Carlo was to be hired as an assistant on most of Heath's bigger movies.

And his luck held: the hunt for acting roles went well. With Henderson talking him up, Heath had relatively little trouble finding work. First came a small-ish role in *Blackrock*, a movie wherein a rape and murder are witnessed by a schoolboy who is then presented with a thorny dilemma: should he keep silent so as to avoid betraying his friend? Heath's part included a scene where another teenager gave him a good thumping. In a different vein altogether there then followed *Paws*, a bubbly animated children's comedy starring Scots actor-comedian Billy Connolly as the voice of the dog. It's been compared, generously, to the blockbuster hit *Beethoven*. The dog knows where a million dollar fortune

can be found. Heath appears in a play within the film, as a student playing William Shakespeare's character Oberon. A strange clash of high and low culture then, this one.

Then came the seemingly compulsory rite of passage for young, attractive Australian actors – a role in the super-successful and durable TV soap *Home and Away*. No shame in this: after all, Heath's friend Guy Pearce and even Kylie Minogue have gone on to great things after appearing in major Aussie soaps – and it paid the rent! As the *Summer Bay* types suffered their daily trials and tribulations, Ledger took a story arc of a few episodes as a dishevelled surfer boy, Scott Irwin, who has a dark, disturbing secret. When framed

for a crime he didn't commit and excluded by the school, he carries out a nasty assault. This was Heath as the bad boy.

A more resonant role was to ensue in 1997 and, significantly, one which brought Heath Ledger attention from the American movie industry for the first time. *Roar* was an American-financed mediaeval fantasy series, produced by the mighty Fox company, and probably inspired by the likes of Mel Gibson's *Braveheart*.

Although filmed in Queensland, *Roar* was set in ancient Britain. The eighteen-year-old Ledger was given the leading role as Conor, a purportedly Celtic prince who wrestled weekly with new, sometimes mythical, enemies with magical

powers. Meanwhile, his main mission was to unite the squabbling clans and repel the invading Roman hordes from the proud island. There was a rather confusingly immortal arch villain, said to have been a soldier present at, and involved in, the crucifixion of Jesus. Heath's dignity was usually veiled only by a Tarzan-like loincloth, and the scriptwriters regularly provided him with a variety of female admirers or adversaries. He was given a young wife who was rather too swiftly (and rashly) killed, which left the story with a few tangled ends it didn't really need so early on. She was played by Keri Russell, the actress who would later find fame in the TV comedy series *Felicity* (for which she won a Golden Globe), as well as the movies *Mission: Impossible 3*, *We Were Soldiers*, and the Adrienne Shelly film *Waitress*. Vera Farmiga, then almost a complete unknown, also featured.

In the States, *Roar* drew initial interest but its ratings soon plummeted. In such a merciless marketplace it would be axed before the entire series had been shown. Its relative failure may have tainted the young Ledger's stock in some industry quarters. It did, however, register him firmly in the consciousness of prospective American employers. It wouldn't be too grandiose to say that, despite not bringing him overnight global celebrity, *Roar* changed Heath's life forever. It gave him a growing following of female fans as well as invaluable experience of working on big-budget sets.

It also found him a girlfriend: he wooed another co-star, Lisa Zane, the sister of *Titanic* star Billy Zane. Lisa was twelve years older than Heath, and a pattern of dating older women began here. So enamoured were the couple with each other that Heath travelled to Los Angeles with Zane. Fox were promoting and encouraging him, and he quickly landed an American agent in Hollywood. *Roar*, however, bore the stigma of failure – dumped on his blameless

shoulders – and job offers did not immediately materialise.

Ironically, it took an Australian movie to get his career back on track again. The film in question was *Two Hands*, directed by Gregor Jordan. Alongside Australian film legend Bryan Brown and another star-to-be, Rose Byrne, Ledger took the lead role in this visceral, heated thriller, sometimes labelled an 'Aussie *Lock Stock & Two Smoking Barrels*', as Jimmy, a small-time suburban Sydney ducker-and-diver, deluding himself that he's on the verge of making the big-time in the crime underworld. Brown's Pando, a genuine crime-lord, tells him to deliver a package of ten thousand dollars, but Jimmy loses it, his focus grabbed and head turned by Byrne's pretty face. Ledger was excellent opposite Byrne, showing us how Jimmy's daily bravado wobbles and cracks when he's made nervous by her proximity. To pay the intimidating Pando back, he is forced to embroil himself in a bigger, riskier bank job.

The film worked, and Ledger shone. He was nominated for a Film Critics Circle of Australia award as best actor, while the Australian Film Institute gave the movie several awards, among them those for direction, music and best supporting actor (Brown).

Gregor Jordan was to go on to make such films as 2001's acclaimed *Buffalo Soldiers* and 2003's *Ned Kelly* (in which he was to re-unite with Ledger as leading man). His most recent film *The Informers*, based on *American Psycho* author Bret Easton Ellis's vastly under-rated book of short stories, was to be the last film of young actor Brad Renfro. In a tragic twist of fate, the troubled Renfro died shortly before Heath did.

Right now, however, *Two Hands* was making the sound of applause ring out. Heath Ledger was making a splash. This time, Hollywood sat up and took notice.

CHAPTER THREE

'Can't Take My Eyes Off You'

THE BREAKTHROUGH ROLE of 1999 came in a sparky, irreverent, cute-teens adaptation of Shakespeare's *The Taming of the Shrew*. 'Fresh, funny, and written in a subtle but clever style,' said the BBC of the Gil Junger-directed *Ten Things I Hate About You*. Penned with much wicked glee by Karen McCullah Lutz and Kirsten Smith, this inconsistent but very funny comedy rather blotted its smart-ass credentials by adopting the tagline: 'How do I loathe thee? Let me count the ways.' Sadly for the producers the Shakespearean sonnet they imagined themselves to be parodying – 'How do I love thee?' – was actually written not by the bard of Avon but by Elizabeth Barrett Browning. But hey, otherwise its literary gags were pretty good.

ABOVE: Heath and Julia Stiles face off with Alison Janney as referee in *Ten Things I Hate About You*

The original play was very loosely adapted. As is the mode in the better teen comedies, students at Padua High School are both frisky and preternaturally articulate. New boy Cameron wants to date sophomore Bianca Stratford, but her father won't let her go out with boys until her older 'shrew' sister Kat (Julia Stiles) does. Catch is, Kat doesn't want to. She likes feminist prose, indie music and non-conformity. So Cameron, and his rival, need to find someone irresistible to her. Enter Heath Ledger as Patrick Verona, the bad-boy rebel with a winning smile who hangs out at pool halls and is rumoured to have eaten a live duck, enjoyed a career in porn, and set fire to a state trooper. Will he and the acerbic Kat want, or be able to, melt each other's resistance and go to the prom together? Or will it be a case of, to quote another unfortunately misguided tagline: 'Romeo, Romeo, get out of my face'?

There's a terrific chemistry between Ledger and Stiles: indeed they were nominated for a Teen Choice Award as Sexiest Love Scene. The entire cast clearly have fun, from rising names Joseph Gordon-Levitt and Gabrielle Union to the peerless Alison Janney (CJ from *The West Wing*) as Ms Perky. For all the mess it gets itself into trying to fuse half a dozen different Shakespeare tropes, the script is dynamite,

loaded with magical quips as Pat and Kat spar and the supporting characters revel in delicious sarcasm and put-downs not generally seen this side of *Buffy the Vampire Slayer* and its subsequent imitators.

Ledger – his fee $100,000 – gets to glower, sing and dance. In a nod to his hero Gene Kelly he has the movie's showstopping scene as he impresses Kat by commandeering the school's outdoor sound system and serenading her by the sports field with the Andy Williams chestnut 'Can't Take My Eyes Off You', as the school's marching band strides and plays alongside him. The band had never actually marched before and were painstakingly trained just for the shot. The broad, likeable scene lodged Ledger in the youth market's brain. He was given an MTV Movie Award nomination for Best Musical Performance, and it was a shock when he didn't win. Interestingly, the original screenplay had called for him to croon The Partridge Family's seventies pop hit 'I Think I Love You', but the Andy Williams karaoke favourite pipped it at the last. Its impact was huge; Heath was now a hot-in-Hollywood heart-throb.

The dialogue helped all the players seem cooler than cool. When a friend quotes Shakespeare, 'Sweet love, renew thy force', Patrick snaps, 'Hey! Don't say shit like that to me.

ABOVE: Heath had the chance to emulate his hero, Gene Kelly, by singing and dancing in *Ten Things I Hate About You*

People can hear you!' On another occasion, finding himself falling in love, he muses, 'What is it with this chick? She has beer-flavoured nipples?'

But it is with Stiles' sceptical Kat that the thrust and parry really takes off.

'Someone still has her panties in a twist,' he says.

'Don't, for one minute,' she replies, 'think that you had any effect whatsoever on my panties.'

'Then what did I have an effect on?' he pushes.

'Other than my upchuck reflex, nothing,' barks Kat.

Ledger's Patrick also enjoys useful asides like, 'Ooh, see that, there? Who needs affection when I have blind hatred?' and 'Leave it to you to use big words when you're smashed.'

Yet he is always aware that he has more than met his match in Kat. 'Some asshole paid me to take out this really great girl,' he confesses to her.

'Is that right?'

'Yeah,' he blushes, 'but I screwed up. I . . . um . . . I fell for her.'

It's a welcome deflation of his previous cocky arrogance.

Kat: 'You are amazingly self-assured. Has anyone ever told you that?'

Patrick: 'I tell myself that every day, actually.'

Ten Things I Hate About You has all the more charm for mostly avoiding sentimentality and maintaining a hip, hilarious pace. Reviews were good. Variety.com reckoned 'Julia Stiles and Aussie transplant Ledger make an assured lead duo', while *The San Francisco Chronicle* called them 'smirky, bright and attractive'. *The New York Times* was less convinced: 'for a bad boy . . . when all's said and done, he seems awfully mild-mannered . . . his is not an act to challenge the transgressive style of Marilyn Manson.'

Despite a minority of detractors *Ten Things . . .* was a sizeable international hit, and more than doubled its costs in US box office ticket sales alone. Heath Ledger was now, to the money-men, a potential marquee name. He was happening. Script offers came flooding in.

Most of them were High School comedies, intent on appeasing the planet's girls by capitalising on Heath's burgeoning pin-up status. His killer smile drew comparisons to Tom Cruise. Yet already, pleased as he was by taking part in a hit and forging a name, Heath was reluctant to pursue that path further. He adamantly advised his agent to reject anything resembling a 'romp'. Intent on avoiding typecasting, he craved serious, respectable, indie parts. Perhaps it was too soon for him to adopt such an attitude.

The studios felt they had no evidence that he could tackle something overtly deeper. While he waited, he settled in Los Angeles, in the Laurel Canyon area. This was one of the more bohemian areas of LA, populated by musicians and artists, and Ledger lived with a few old, trusted friends from Australia. He had re-met a former acquaintance while attuning to LA life: Christina Cauchi, an attractive model, became his new girlfriend. They set up home together.

Man cannot live on one hit movie alone, however, and funds dwindled. There followed close to a year of what Ledger has referred to as 'poverty' (possibly a slight exaggeration with a dash of poetic license), during which he survived, he claimed, on noodles and water. The twenty-

year-old could have snapped up a generic hunk role but, not for the last time, he refused to compromise.

His patience was rewarded when, in 2000, he won a part in his next big movie, *The Patriot*. Primarily a Mel Gibson vehicle, directed by Roland Emmerich, who went on to make *10,000 B.C.*, it was a huge hit. Yet Ledger so nearly blew it – his first audition was a disaster. Having taken time out, Heath had lost his confidence, despite the praise for *Ten Things…* Previously his relative lack of formal training and his inexperience hadn't bothered the bold young man, but now he found himself jittery and nervous.

He went to the audition with Emmerich, who was already a very big name on the back of *Independence Day* and *Godzilla*,

LEFT: Heath fluffed his first audition for *The Patriot* but was lucky enough to be given a second chance

ABOVE: Heath was ultimately chosen for the role above two hundred other hopefuls, including Jake Gyllenhaal, with whom he would later star in *Brokeback Mountain*

and fell to pieces. He walked out, embarrassed.

'I'm the worst auditioner,' Heath once said in 2001. 'Really, really bad. I mean, you're being judged . . . and I'm just so aware of it that it consumes me. I can't relax, I'm tied in knots. So the voice is very taut and tense. You're so aware that you're acting, because you're sitting across from this lady with a piece of paper who's going, "I'm. Going. To. Shoot. You. If. You. Don't . . . blah, blah, blah" in this emotionless voice. It's foul! I hate it.'

Good fortune intervened again. A casting director who knew he had talent, and was aware that females seemed to love the Australian, stalled the director and called him back for a second audition. There were over two hundred applicants, including Paul Walker and one Jake Gyllenhaal, later to be Heath's co-star in *Brokeback Mountain* and

godfather to his only child, who had several auditions but Ledger impressed this time around. Eventually the role (as Mel Gibson's son) was between Ryan Philippe and himself: Ledger took it. Happy to see a paycheque, he loyally spent money on his friends and gave over his per diem payments to his old mentor Martin Henderson, who at this stage was struggling for meaningful work.

The Patriot built on the gung-ho revenge passions of fellow Australian Gibson's biggest hit *Braveheart*. Only this time Mel wasn't a Scot hating the English, but an American loathing the Brits. Needless to say, the film fared less well in the UK than in other territories. Set in South Carolina in 1776, it cast Gibson as farmer Benjamin Martin, a haunted, guilt-ridden veteran of the French-Indian war who wants no part in any further conflicts if at all possible. Such tranquillity

LEFT: Although he had eschewed firearms instruction at school, Heath had to learn how to use an old-fashioned musket for *The Patriot*

ABOVE: One reviewer said of Heath's performance alongside Mel Gibson that he had 'the talent and the looks to become a major star'

is, of course, impossible on the threshold of the American Revolution. His two eldest sons, Gabriel (Ledger) and Thomas, are excited by the prospect of a war with Britain. When South Carolina joins the battle, Gabriel, keen to end slavery, eagerly signs up without his father's permission. The chief villain of the piece, Colonel Tavington, cleverly played by Jason Isaacs (although Kevin Spacey had been first choice), captures Gabriel and sentences him to hang. He then kills Thomas as he tries to save Gabriel, in front of Benjamin. His brutality – not to mention the burning down of his house – brings out the vengeful beast in Benjamin, who cranks up the bloody carnage with some patented guerilla tactics. You can't help but root for him and his makeshift militia of peasants and slaves as noisy battle rages. As respite, Gabriel has a few touching quiet scenes with his father along the way, and a love interest in Lisa Bremer. Joely Richardson also stars.

The New York Times raved over Gibson, almost accidentally eulogising Ledger while in full flow.

'He (Gibson) is an astonishing actor for someone whose technique all seems to come from the outside . . . he relates to the performers playing his children, even the somewhat remote Heath Ledger, who plays Gabriel, the oldest son and the one most like his dad. In their scenes together, Gibson almost seems to be directing Ledger onscreen, and the younger actor responds with an exasperated bashfulness that makes him less cool and more likeable.'

Similarly, *Rolling Stone* loved Gibson's 'unleashing of his demons': 'Himself the parent of seven, he brings ardour and complexity to this conflicted father. His scenes with Heath Ledger – the Aussie newcomer has the talent and looks to become a major star – provide an intimacy that holds an overlong film together against the winds of bombast . . .'

There was interesting tittle-tattle behind the scenes.

ABOVE: In interviews Heath affirmed his ambition by maintaining that he felt he could always improve on a performance

ABOVE: Showing some style at Bowlrmor Lanes in New York at the premiere party for *Boys And Girls* in 2000

Screenwriter Robert Rodat had been through seventeen drafts, and Harrison Ford had passed on most of them. There had been six children in the story before Gibson – father of seven – requested one more. And when Gibson was paid his super-size fee, there wasn't enough money left to hire Kevin Spacey. As for Heath, he performed all his own stunts. There's a scene in the film just prior to the ambush where Gibson advises Ledger to 'aim small, miss small'. That is: if you aim at a man and miss, you miss the man. But if you aim at, say, a button, and miss, you still hit the man. The actors were taught this tidbit by technical advisor Mark Baker, while learning how to shoot a muzzle-loading rifle, and Gibson liked it so much he tossed it casually into the scene.

Perhaps the promotion of the film was over-zealous. Posters and ads roared out wild-eyed stuff like: 'What would you do if they destroyed your home, threatened your family?

Where would you draw the line?' and 'Before they were soldiers, they were family. Before they were legends, they were heroes. Before there was a nation, there was a fight for freedom.' It all made you want to plead with the person in charge to calm down. 'Some things are worth fighting for' was another of its hard-sell pitches.

The Patriot divided critics down the middle (except the Brits, who hated it to a man), and collected Oscar nominations for just cinematography, sound and John Williams' score. On the plus side, Ledger won a Blockbuster Entertainment Award for favourite male newcomer. It had undoubtedly been a valuable building block for him.

Still, there were blips around the corner. He almost got the role of The Devil in the Peter Hyams-helmed Arnold Schwarzenegger film *End Of Days* (losing out to Gabriel Byrne, perhaps mercifully) and then narrowly missed out on a part in the much talked-about TV sci-fi series *Roswell*.

LEFT: While he took his craft very seriously, Heath was a party animal and enjoyed the showbiz social scene

LEFT: A different party, a different black leather jacket, this one on display at the premiere of *The Cell* in London in 2000

Here he'd tussled for the part of Max Evans, one of the quartet of super-powered human-alien hybrids. The Fox producers however, having long memories and a desire to shift blame, harboured reservations about him after getting their fingers burned with mediaeval series *Roar*. And then Heath made what you might describe as a poor decision. Still torn over what constituted a 'serious' role and what didn't, he turned down the title role in *Spider Man*. Which Tobey Maguire gratefully accepted (the franchise has proven a world-beating hit).

You have to pause here to imagine how different a route Ledger's career may have taken if he had, for better or worse, played Spidey, the web-slinging wonder. Playing a comic book hero can either rocket you to the A-list or dump you in the gutter, often depending on factors outside your control. That was one risk he wasn't prepared to accept.

Heath gave an interview at around this time where he said: 'I feel like I'm wasting time if I repeat myself. I can't say I'm proud of my work. It's the same with everything I do. The day I say "It's good" is the day I should start doing something else . . .'

Another mooted role was, implausibly, as an English football fan in Sardinia, Italy, in a planned movie named *Calcio*, but it's said the Weinstein brothers, Harvey in particular, didn't at this stage fancy the cut of his jib. They were to change their minds soon enough when it came to casting *The Four Feathers*.

There was, happily, a big movie on the horizon for Ledger. Whether it was quite the kind of movie he'd been holding out for is debatable. Then again, whether it turned out to be quite the kind of movie everyone involved had intended it to be when they started it is debatable, too. *A Knight's Tale* is a rather bizarre one-off.

CHAPTER FOUR

'He Will Rock You'

SPEAKING TO *VANITY FAIR* in August 2000, Heath Ledger said,
'I only do this because I'm having fun. The day I stop having fun,
I'll just walk away. I wasn't going to have fun doing a teen movie
again . . .' That established, he continued, 'I don't want to do this
for the rest of my life . . . I don't want to spend the rest of my youth
doing this in this industry. There's so much I want to discover.'
Yet his next movie *A Knight's Tale*, to Heath's chagrin, made
great play of his good looks, a poster campaign targeted
directly at young, impressionable females hollering in big bold
sledgehammer print: 'He Will Rock You'. Ledger felt it placed
far too much emphasis on his own shoulders, but it worked:
a strange, funny, disjointed movie grossed over $56 million
and confirmed him in Hollywood as a *bona fide* star who
could launch a film. Even a decidedly odd one.

LEFT: Heath with Shannyn Sossamon,
his leading lady in *A Knight's Tale*

Brian Helgeland was hot, having written the Curtis Hanson hit and Oscar magnet *L.A. Confidential*, starring Australian actors Russell Crowe and Guy Pearce, plus Kevin Spacey and Kim Basinger. Helgeland had himself nabbed an Oscar for the screenplay. So everybody expected quality and depth from his next venture, which he chose to direct himself. Few anticipated a colourful, silly, adventure romp set in fourteenth-century Europe and involving hunky knights in armour, cute damsels, jousting, wonderfully incongruous musical interludes and a highly tenuous link to the famed *Canterbury Tales* of English Lit syllabus favourite Geoffrey Chaucer.

Over an inspired, slightly insane, rock soundtrack featuring David Bowie, Queen, Thin Lizzy, AC/DC, Bachman Turner Overdrive, Sly Stone and Smokey Robinson, Ledger was cast as the hero, William Thatcher, an underdog squire with comedy sidekicks who included Paul Bettany's loudly camp Chaucer, *The Full Monty*'s Mark Addy as Roland and Alan Tudyk's Wat. Thatcher graduates to knight status illegally, using documents forged by Chaucer. He wins jousting contests, gaining a fan club and contending with a nasty adversary (Rufus Sewell) to win the hand of the beauteous maiden Lady Jocelyn (Shannyn Sossamon).

Speaking to *Access Hollywood* in August 2000, Heath laughed, 'It's a little uncomfortable doing love scenes in armour but, you know, when the heat's on, the heat's on.'

'Heath Ledger is a likeably vulnerable hero,' opined *The Observer* and William Thatcher certainly had more than a few lines designed to display his honour and nobility. When Jocelyn sighs, 'Damn your pride, William,' he replies, 'My pride is the only thing they can't take away from me.'

When Roland says, 'God love you, William,' he responds, 'I know, I know – because no-one else will.' Among his other love-me pleas are, 'Love has given me wings so I must fly' and 'If I could ask God one thing, it would be to stop the moon. Stop the moon and make this night and your beauty last forever.'

But we're making it sound earnest and pompous: *A Knight's Tale*, for all its flaws, is neither of those. It's daft, boisterous fun. Heath dances again. *The Guardian*'s Peter Bradshaw nailed it: 'Oh to have been a fly on the wall at the pitch meeting for this movie . . .' ran his review. '*Gladiator* meets *Monty Python and the Holy Grail* . . . a deeply silly film . . .

it's somehow very entertaining, and its bizarre in-your-face anachronisms are carried off with such insouciance, such cheerful effrontery, that you can't help indulging them.' As Ledger had feared would be the case, he, like many other reviewers, described Heath as 'Hollywood's hunk of the moment, with his tousled beach-blond hair.' Roger Ebert called the film 'a stout showcase for Ledger, a new Aussie gladiator . . . Helgeland employs Ledger's looks and charm to solid effect but doesn't let him hog the show. A dumb summer movie with smarts.' *Rolling Stone* described Heath as 'the next big thing on the Aussie sex symbol front.'

A Knight's Tale was winning froth: again Ledger found himself nominated at the lighter end of the awards spectrum. He and Shannyn Sossamon were up for Best Kiss at the MTV Movie Awards, and Best Musical Sequence for their striking dance routine to David Bowie's 'Golden Years'. He also picked up a Teen Choice Award nomination. Not the heavy-duty grown-up honours he was pining for, but all grist to the publicity mill. Plus Heath collected a healthy fee of $3 million.

ABOVE: Heath with Shannyn Sossamon at the US premiere of *A Knight's Tale*

ABOVE: Heather Graham, whom Heath met while filming the movie in Prague, accompanies him at the premiere of *A Knight's Tale*

It surely can't have been frustration at the role that caused Ledger to knock out one of Brian Helgeland's front teeth during rehearsal of a jousting move – the only jousting injury on the entire set, and one from which the unlucky Helgeland's mouth took months to recover.

The younger William, in flashback, was played by an actor who had different coloured eyes to Ledger, but Helgeland thought asking him to wear contact lenses would be too precious. A stunt double was used on occasion, and was once knocked unconscious.

The film – or its promotional campaign – did draw controversy when the studio, Columbia, were found to have rather foolishly invented an entirely fictitious quote from a non-existent reviewer (a 'David Manning') for its posters. It seems incredible that they'd stoop to such depths as the film surely wasn't that desperate and, once exposed, the shame tainted many filmgoers' enjoyment.

Still, a hit's a hit, and Heath had to be happy with his hard day's knight. He had further cause to be upbeat: when filming *A Knight's Tale* in Prague, he met actress Heather Graham, who was on location shooting *From Hell* (the Hughes Brothers' chiller) with Johnny Depp in the same city. Graham, also well-known for *Boogie Nights*, *Two Girls and a Guy* and *Austin Powers*, may have been struggling with an Irish accent on set, but she and Ledger fell easily into romance. She was nine years Ledger's senior and Heath was to admit that the age difference was part of the attraction.

'I prefer to date older women,' Ledger once said, not, of course, specifically referring to Heather (that would not be gallant) but to an emerging pattern, 'because they don't try to act older like younger girls – they try to act younger.'

The starry Ledger-Graham romance ran from October 2000 to June 2001. In the latter year, Ledger was named one of *People* magazine's Fifty Most Beautiful People. He was

ABOVE: Heath with cinematographer Robert Richardson and director Shekhar Kapur on the set of *The Four Feathers*

also to appear as a men's fashion judge at the Melbourne Cup Carnival in November 2001.

His next shoot, although the film was actually released after *Monster's Ball* (about which more shortly), again cast him as the dashing hero on horseback. *The Four Feathers* was a remake – in fact, the seventh version in total – of a 1915 ripping yarn by A.E.W. Mason. Zoltan Korda's 1939 take on the imperialist adventure was probably the template; Don Sharp's 1978 reworking was also an influence. The twenty-first century big-budget updating was directed by Shekhar Kapur, famous for the *Elizabeth* movies starring Cate Blanchett. It was to turn into a very troubled production, its narrative wobbly, its mostly American and Australian actors wrestling with upper-crust British accents. Cast alongside Ledger were Kate Hudson (*Almost Famous*),

Wes Bentley *(American Beauty)*, Djimon Hounsou, Michael Sheen and *Spooks* star Rupert Penry-Jones.

Ledger, paid a reported two million dollars for the movie, was cast as Harry Faversham, who is labelled a dastardly coward when he refuses to fight with the British Army in the Sudan in 1875, wishing to stay with his beloved (Hudson). Soon enough, however, he follows his regiment to the war zone and proves his heroism by saving their lives almost single-handedly several times over.

The feathers of the title are given to him when he's deemed a coward. Good job he redeems himself. His best, most soulful speech, and the one which allows Ledger the most scope for reflection, muses:

'When something like this happens you are lost. You don't know where you are any more and what you're capable

ABOVE: Heath had another chance to display his sporting prowess during the filming of *The Four Feathers*

RIGHT: Playing the male lead of Harry Faversham, Ledger was reported to have earned $2 million for *The Four Feathers*

of. Unless I do something this is always how people will remember me. A feather. And that is how I will always see myself: a coward. All I know is that I can't live with myself like this.'

This was a peculiar choice of movie by its makers. For all the script's attempts at being politically correct, British gung-ho imperialist adventures was hardly a hot topic. The issues with direction and production meant it became an expensive failure, a fleet of bright young stars hung out to dry, its release delayed. *Lawrence of Arabia*, it wasn't. 'Clunking dialogue, insecure action,' noted one reviewer, while *The Guardian* praised Ledger for doing his own stunts and riding, but added, 'It loses urgency and focus and becomes, well, a bit boring.'

Another blow landed on Ledger: craving the role opposite Nicole Kidman in Baz Luhrmann's glamorous musical epic *Moulin Rouge*, he was told he seemed too young to play opposite Kidman. Ewan McGregor took the part. There was, however, a valuable gift granted to Ledger by the

Kapur project, and he didn't stay still long enough for the problems of *The Four Feathers* to upset his career. On set he'd befriended fellow up-and-coming actor Wes Bentley, who told Ledger he was on the brink of exhaustion and would be happy to extricate himself from his next movie commitment, which was set to begin practically as soon as *The Four Feathers* finished. He asked Heath if he'd be interested in taking over the role from him, and set the relevant wheels in motion. With such short notice, the studio were content with the trade-off. Heath had spotted that it was an intriguing role in a potentially riveting film.

It was, of course, *Monster's Ball*, directed by Marc Forster, and starring Billy Bob Thornton along with eventual Oscar-winner Halle Berry. Ledger's role in this moving and powerful picture was relatively small but absolutely vital to the unique tone and atmosphere. It showed him in a new light. More profoundly, it gave him the opportunity to reveal a new darkness within himself.

ABOVE: Heath's 2003 movie, *The Order*,
was a complete washout

CHAPTER FIVE

Shock Tactics

MONSTER'S BALL TOOK ITS TITLE from the antiquated
British term given to a party thrown in jail for a condemned
man, just before he's executed. The darkest and most compelling
film with which Heath Ledger had so far been involved, it was set
in Georgia in the Southern US. It begins in a bleak penitentiary
with Lawrence Musgrove (Sean 'Puffy' Combs) awaiting his date
in the electric chair. The exact nature of his crime is withheld,
but we know that he's been on Death Row for eleven years.
Hank Grotowski (Billy Bob Thornton) is a taciturn, dedicated
prison guard. He works alongside his inexperienced, sensitive,
warder son, Sonny (Ledger), and lives at home with his father
(Peter Boyle), formerly a guard, now just an ill and bitter racist.
Hank and Sonny have a strange, dysfunctional rapport.
They share a hooker. Hank is given the duty of executing
Musgrove. He's a professional, stoic, steely.

ABOVE: Heath escorts the condemned man, Sean Coombs, along with Billy Bob Thornton in *Monster's Ball*

Leticia (Halle Berry) is Musgrove's widow. Soon Hank, also a widower since his wife killed herself, has a new personal tragedy to match hers: he feels Sonny lets him down by vomiting while escorting the condemned man to the chair. Mirroring Leticia's disappointment with her obese son, he can't hide his bitterness at Sonny's behaviour and treats him harshly. Then, in a shocking scene barely halfway through the film, the humiliated Sonny kills himself, in front of his father and grandfather.

Hank, distraught, leaves the prison service, buying a gas station. Meanwhile, Leticia's home is repossessed, and her own son is killed by a hit-and-run car. Perhaps it's not such a twist, then, that when the pair, both poor, finally meet, they fall in love, clutching at a small chance of some happiness. Their relationship is, in this context, controversially inter-racial. It's also very passionate and steamy, involving some electric sex scenes. Sooner or later though, surely Hank will learn that Leticia is the widow of the man whose life he ended?

It's a stark, uncompromising, lacerating film, awash with human misery and despair. Capital punishment, racism and graphic sex don't make for cosy family viewing. It's also quite brilliant, with some truly great performances. *Premiere* magazine deemed it massively over-rated, few viewers would concur. Made for a tiny $4 million budget, with the chief actors pretty much doing it for love, it had survived six years of the script languishing in 'development'.

Way back, it had been mooted as starring Robert De Niro and being directed by Sean Penn. Vanessa Williams turned down the Halle Berry role; Queen Latifah and Angela Bassett had been considered for it. Wes Bentley may well, with hindsight, have regretted handing the Sonny role over to Ledger.

Despite its furiously feel-bad tendencies, it won Milo Addica and Will Rokos an Oscar nomination for best screenplay. Famously, Halle Berry won the Oscar for Best Actress in a Leading Role and wept a lot during her acceptance speech. Billy Bob Thornton should have won

ABOVE: Heath made a huge impact in his role as prison guard, Sonny, despite only being in *Monster's Ball* for forty minutes

every award going. The director, Forster, moved on to all-round success, from *Finding Neverland* to *The Kite Runner*, most recently helming the new Bond movie *Quantum of Solace*.

As for Heath Ledger, he may have been overshadowed by the central couple (as anybody would have been), but his heartbreaking performance sent word that this young heart-throb had a lot more depth than most had previously suspected. It showed he didn't care about looking pretty: this was strong, painful stuff. In taking a non-lead role, he hit on a way of digging deeper into a brand of human nature. Criticised by his father, stung by his grandfather, Sonny isn't cut out for the gruesome work he has to undertake at the prison. Perhaps he had more in common with his mother than his father. His suicide, which comes as a real shock, serves to make Hank reconsider his every value, and scramble for redemption. Like the film, his performance is about shades of grey, avoiding the predictable or sentimental.

The uneasy relationshop between Sonny and Hank manifests itself in a tough, crucial exchange between son and father.

'You hate me,' cries Sonny. 'You hate me, don't you? Answer me! You hate me, don't you?'

Hank drawls, 'Yes, I hate you. I always have.'

'Well,' says Sonny, with something approaching resignation, 'I've always loved you . . .'

Reviews recognised Ledger's contribution. *Rolling Stone* praised a 'de-glammed' actor. Another critic acclaimed his 'short but intense appearance – he's in the film less than forty minutes . . . Ledger pumps the lonely character full of repressed anger and disappointment, simultaneously resenting his father and seeking his approval.'

When I interviewed the likeable and candid Billy Bob Thornton in London a few years ago, he showed a fine understanding of the film's strengths. 'It's sort of ironic, y'know, that people tease me or even clap me on the back about that raw, honest sex scene,' he said. 'They see me on the street and go, "Woah, Halle Berry, check it out!" But

ABOVE: One of the central themes of Monster's Ball was the relationship between Heath as Sonny and Billy Bob Thornton as his father, Hank

I remember when we shot it, it was everything but fun. It was very heavy. It was a scene about loneliness more than anything else. And we pulled it off. A sense of desperation came across. It wasn't gratuitous.

'There was a heavy, heavy mood on set throughout the film. We all knew we were making something important. Okay, not important on a grand scale – like, we're not solving world hunger here. But in terms of personal relationships, racism and real life. It dealt with the sins of the father, how responsible we are. If you have children then whatever you do is going to reflect on them and affect their lives. So we all took it seriously. I'm not saying it wasn't a good experience, Marc Forster's a wonderful guy, but the tone was, rightly, sombre when it needed to be.'

It certainly was.

Heath Ledger's next career move was, again, imperfect. Now living in the West Village in New York and re-united with old flame Christina Cauchi (after the demise of his affair with Heather Graham, which had attracted the attention of the paparazzi too much for the pair's liking), he flew to Rome to film the next offering from *A Knight's Tale*

director Brian Helgeland, *The Sin Eater*. Despite friends from Helgeland's last film Shannyn Sossamon and Mark Addy appearing among the cast, and Peter Weller apparently doing extensive research into old religious rituals and histrionics, *The Sin Eater* – aka *The Order* – was a chronic misfire. Histrionics was all it had going for it. 'A load of risible, scarcely intelligible piffle, in which a maverick priest goes from New York to Rome to investigate the death of the head of his dubious order,' scoffed *The Observer*. 'How this came to be made and considered fit for release are twin mysteries.' And that was far from the worst review!

The plot confused everybody. To attempt to explain it: Alex Bernier (Ledger) is a member of an arcane order of priests, the 'Carolingians'. When the head of the Carolingians dies, Alex visits Rome to investigate the mysterious circumstances surrounding his demise. The body bears weird marks on the chest which we learn might be the sign of a Sin Eater. The Sin Eater, named William Eden, was played by Benno Furmann, who replaced Vincent Cassel when the French actor left after three weeks due to 'creative differences'. Eden claims to be five hundred years

ABOVE: By the time he had finished making *Monster's Ball*, Heath had also split with Heather Graham (seen here with him in London in 2001) and had returned to former love Christina Cauchi

old. He offers demonic absolution, last rites and a path to heaven outside the jurisdiction of the church. This entails his devouring bread and wine off naked bodies while mumbling in Arabaic.

Alex enlists the aid of his old friend Father Thomas (Addy) and a disturbed (aren't we all, by now) artist, Mara Sinclair (Sossamon), upon whom he once performed an exorcism. He's soon knee deep in slasher-horror special effects: knives flying out of walls, and suchlike. Test audiences laughed when they weren't supposed to – they thought the 'sins' leaving bodies resembled 'calamari' – and the release date was severely delayed while scenes were re-shot.

Despite hard-sell ads pitching the designer-stubbled Ledger's moody looks and saying 'Unleash the power!' and 'Every soul has its price' and (a very clumsy) 'Behind the disguise of good lies the soul of evil', this was a doomed project. On viewing it, it was hard to believe Helgeland could also pen smart scripts like *Mystic River*. It sidelined his directing career.

Around the same time, similarly-themed Satanic-horror movies like *Stigmata* (starring Patricia Arquette), *Lost Souls* (starring Winona Ryder) and *Bless The Child* (starring Kim Basinger) also tanked. Perhaps it was simply the wrong time to tap into the themes the phenomenally popular *The Da Vinci Code* was to exploit before too long. 'There (may be) a market for movies with troubled, hunky young priests investigating Satanic cults at the heart of the Vatican,' pondered *The Guardian*'s Peter Bradshaw, before dismissing the film. BBCi's Nev Pierce remarked, 'From the scarily overrated *The Exorcist* to laugh-starved comedy *We're No Angels*, pictures involving priests often deserve damnation.' He went on to bemoan its 'cinematic cretinism'.

In March 2003, *The Hollywood Reporter* made a valid point. 'Aussie actor Heath Ledger is still chasing a hit. A fixture on magazine covers and drawing all kinds of heat, he's yet to go over the top at the box office . . .'

That wasn't going to happen with his next movie either, but this was largely a labour of love for Ledger, who expressed his discontent: he'd hit, he felt, 'a plateau of nothing.' Heath fled from Helgeland's hammy horror to take an assignment back in Australia, and worked again there with director Gregor Jordan, who'd given him his

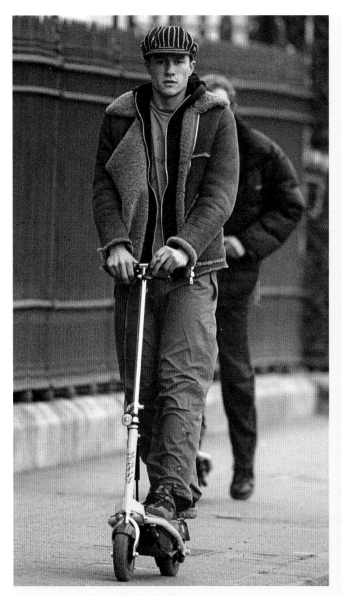

LEFT: Heath with Shannyn Sossamon in *The Order*
ABOVE: Trying out a novel way of getting around
London on a motorised scooter

ABOVE: Heath fitted the role of Ned Kelly perfectly – he even fitted into Ned
Kelly's original suit of armour

break in *Two Hands*. To prove his commitment, Ledger took a fee of just £50,000 for the movie, a hit in Australia but not elsewhere. The subject matter was always going to intrigue Australians. It was *Ned Kelly*.

Ned Kelly, written by John Michael McDonagh and based on Robert Drewe's book *Our Sunshine*, told the favourite Australian fable of Kelly, the 'legendary outlaw', the 'bushranger and icon'. Mick Jagger, of all people, had tried the role in 1975. Now Heath was cast as a local anti-hero, oddly looking a lot like Russell Crowe on the posters and promo material. 'You can kill a man but not a legend,' they said. 'The British Empire branded them outlaws, the oppressed called them heroes.' What was it with the combo of Heath, horseback, and cursing the British colonialists?

The film was flooded with Australian actors. Geoffrey Rush played Superintendent Francis Hare, chasing Kelly. Kelly's love interest, Julia Cook, was played by Naomi Watts, and Rachel Griffiths was among those cameo-ing. British rising star Orlando Bloom was Joe Byrne, Kelly's favoured sidekick.

Ned Kelly is Oz's Robin Hood, although, as one review pointed out, he was a 'cop-killer, bank-robber and all-round anarchy icon.' Ledger's bass voiceover 'showed a taste for bombastic autobiography' but both the film and Heath's performance were generally quite well received. 'After the slightly soft results of *A Knight's Tale* and the disappointing *The Four Feathers*,' wrote *The Hollywood Reporter*, 'Ledger stays on horseback but leads the charge in a far

ABOVE: 'You can kill a man, but you can't kill a legend' was used as a prmotional slogan for *Ned Kelly*

more accomplished film . . . directed with a mix of lyricism and muscular energy . . .' *Ned Kelly* mixed the traditional Hollywood Western conventions of gunplay, horseback chases, bank robberies, honour, loyalty and betrayal, with a genuine Australian consciousness. 'Sentimentalised but watchable,' said *The Guardian*. 'Ledger as Kelly morphs from beardless Irish youth into a ferocious, devious, natural leader of men with a chin-in-chest-out strut.' *The Reporter* was also enthusiastic: 'Ledger is the epitome of rugged rebelliousness but tempers his taciturn restraint with a welcome humour and sensitivity.' *Time Out* thought the film 'stuck uneasily between romantic myth-making and historical accountability.'

As Ned, Ledger relishes some stirring speeches. Confronted by pursuing adversary Hare (Rush), whom he has led on a merry dance across the outback, he asks, 'Wasn't this the challenge of your whole life, Superintendent Hare? A feather in your cap? You can't catch me, you don't have a hope of catching me, so you take my friends instead. Over one hundred men arrested, stuck in stinking cells without trial while their crops perish in the fields. And guess what? Not one of 'em caves in and tries to claim the reward. Not one of 'em. They loved me the same and hated you all the more, didn't they? Did you really think I was gonna let 'em all rot?'

He can be dry as well as righteous. 'I've never shot a

ABOVE: Committed to making the movie rather than furthering
his career, Heath's fee for *Ned Kelly* was just £50,000

ABOVE: Heath with rising star Orlando Bloom on the set of *Ned Kelly*

ABOVE: *Ned Kelly* earned Heath Best Actor nominations in
Australia but was not widely seen elsewhere

man,' he declares on another occasion. 'But if I do, so help
me, God, you'll be the first.'

Ledger was pleased, on home turf, to pick up Best Actor
nominations from both the Australian Film Institute and the
Film Critics Circle of Australia. *Time Out*, however, deemed
his performance 'self-consciously heroic' and lacking 'a sense
of wildness.' He 'makes Ned a decent but ultimately rather
dull underdog.' Perhaps they missed one sense in which he
was made to play the role. When Heath tried on Ned Kelly's
original iron armour, it fitted him perfectly.

Ledger told the *Sydney Morning Herald*, 'It was quite eerie
actually. We're the same height and same body weight. He

was skinny because he was starving. I'm skinny because I
don't go to the gym.'

To this day the armour is on display at the State Library
of Victoria. The blood-stained green sash given to Ned after
he saved a boy from drowning is in a museum in Benalla.
The film's world premiere was held two blocks from where
Kelly was hanged.

There was another important development during
the Ned Kelly shoot. *Home and Away* veterans Ledger and
Naomi Watts began an affair, with Ledger leaving Christina
Cauchi. Eleven years older than Ledger, the fast-rising (after
years in the industry) Watts had recently co-starred with

ABOVE: Heath with Naomi Watts at the press conference to launch *Ned Kelly* in Melbourne in 2003

ABOVE: Former *Home and Away* star Watts began a two-year romance with Heath during the *Ned Kelly* shoot

Ledger's old friend Martin Henderson in Gore Verbinski's *The Ring*. Prior to that she'd excelled in her break-out role as Betty Elms in David Lynch's mesmerising *Mulholland Drive*. She was soon to be Oscar-nominated for Alejandro Gonzalez Inarritu's *21 Grams* and land a coveted role in Peter Jackson's *King Kong*. The romance drew media fuss which neither party really enjoyed. The tabloids loved it, making great play of the age difference. Ledger's discomfort with the attention can be discerned in a comment he made about film premieres and what it felt like to walk down a red carpet, flashbulbs popping, microphones thrust into one's bewildered face.

'Like diving into an Olympic pool, swimming the length underwater, then emerging gasping for breath. It's so noisy that it's quiet, you can't hear; the flashlights are so blinding that it's dark, you can't see.'

Nonetheless, Ledger and Watts maintained a reasonably lengthy relationship, from August 2002 to May 2004. Another 'older woman' for him, but one of the coolest, most talented and most attractive actresses of our times. Born in Kent, England, she moved to North Wales with her mother as a child. Her family brought her to Sydney when she was fourteen. Her father, a sound engineer for rock legends Pink Floyd, died when she was seven. She began to

LEFT AND ABOVE: Heath and Naomi Watts attempting to avoid the attentions of the press while visiting Clovely Beach, Sydney

model and act. Her debut role, on *Home and Away*, was as a paraplegic – a long way from fleeing the hairy clutches of *King Kong*. On the set of John Duigan's *Flirting*, she became best friends with Nicole Kidman. Thousands of auditions in LA followed before the off-the-wall David Lynch triumph, *Mulholland Drive*, which won her countless awards. Since then, other fine films have included Merchant Ivory's *Le Divorce*, John Curran's *We Don't Live Here Anymore*, David O. Russell's *I Heart Huckabees*, David Cronenberg's *Eastern Promises*, Michael Haneke's *Funny Games*, Niels Mueller's *The Assassination of Richard Nixon*, and Scott Coffey's confessional cult classic *Ellie Parker*. In 2005 she was to meet actor/director Liev Schrieber, and in 2007 they had their first child together.

For now though, Watts and Ledger had to duck and dive to avoid the paws of the press. Ledger kept moving, all the more turned off 'celebrity' by the experience.

He was considered for the role of Kar in *Bulletproof Monk*, but shrewdly turned it down. The role went to Seann William Scott. More surprisingly, and riskily, he didn't grab a role discussed with Oliver Stone – that of Alexander in the notorious big-league epic. Colin Farrell snapped it up, to star alongside Angelina Jolie and Anthony Hopkins.

You may think Ledger was foolish to pass up such a high-profile role, but only if you haven't had to sit through *Alexander*, which is a debacle. Employing the shock tactics with which Heath continued to defy traditional expectations, he once again chose to go lower profile – and almost unrecognisable – as the blissed-out Californian surfer guru Skip Engblom in *Lords of Dogtown*.

CHAPTER SIX

'It's Not Magic, It's Just Shiny'

'HEATH LEDGER IS FLAMBOYANTLY funny and alive as Z-Boys guru Skip Engblom,' purred *Rolling Stone* as *Lords of Dogtown* thrilled its target audience. The sports-loving Heath looked decidedly different and clearly enjoyed indulging himself away from the star-maker machinery. A hymn to what Avril Lavigne might call skater boys, this was writer Stacey Peralta's fictional adaptation of his own 2001 documentary *Dogtown and Z-Boys*, about a skateboard team who rose from obscurity to cult stardom. Directorial duties shifted from David Fincher of *Fight Club* fame to rock shouter Fred Durst before landing with Catherine Hardwicke, hot on the back of her hit *Thirteen*.

LEFT: Heath enjoyed indulging his passion for skateboarding in *Lords of Dogtown*

ABOVE: In *Lords of Dogtown*, Heath played the
spaced-out owner of a surf shop, Skip

ABOVE: Heath's character was based on the real-life Skip Engblom,
who was thrilled with his portrayal in the movie

It's the late Seventies, and spaced-out stoner Skip – an anti-hero, a social misfit – owns a surf shop. He recruits local boys to set up a competitive skating team in Dogtown, Santa Monica, California. The skateboarders become known as the Z-Boys. They perfect their craft in the empty swimming pools of unsuspecting suburban home-owners, ultimately pioneering an exciting new sport. 'They came from nothing to change everything' blazed the posters.

When Catherine Hardwicke fell during the rehearsal of one elaborate skateboarding move and was knocked briefly unconscious, she woke to see her cast smiling and saying, 'Welcome to the club. That's what this is like.' The film had a relaxed, likeably sloppy feel, making shrewd asides on friendship and fame, and an ensemble including Emile Hirsch (later to excel in Sean Penn's *Into the Wild*), Nikki Reed (who burst onto the scene in *Thirteen*), Johnny Knoxville and Rebecca De Mornay appeared to have as good a time as Ledger did. Although the subject matter and milieu may not have translated everywhere (in some

territories the title was amended to *American Knights*, or *Dogtown Boys*), the movie did well, helped by a soundtrack featuring Jimi Hendrix and Neil Young. It wasn't without faults: there was a fair amount of product placement and in-jokes, as well as a rather hagiographical belief that these boys were demi-gods who must be worshipped by all girls. Youthfulness was its chief strength, however, and the cameras capture the whoosh and thrill of sporting endeavour with giddying swoops and dives.

As a bonus, there was a Central Ohio Film Critics Association award for Ledger as Actor of the Year (this took into account his other releases that year), and a Teen Choice Award nomination. Perhaps the highest accolade was that the real Skip Engblom had wanted Heath to play him, and was exuberant at the result.

Characters in the whip-smart 2001 comedy *Josie and the Pussycats* had affectionately compared Heath to Matt Damon. Now he was to pair up with the ever-busy Damon for *The Brothers Grimm*, a typically convoluted Terry

ABOVE: Part of the *Dogtown* team – Johnny Knoxville, producer John Linson, Heath, Rebecca De Mornay and writer Stacy Peralta, a former professional skateboarder

Gilliam production. As seems often to be the case with the unlucky, fairy-tale-obsessed Gilliam's movies, things did not run overly smoothly, and it carries the reputation of an ambitious flop.

MGM originally funded the movie, but suddenly pulled out, and the Weinstein brothers moved in. By June 2004 Gilliam was at loggerheads with Robert Weinstein over the film's final cut, and put it on hold for six months while he went to make another film, *Tideland*. He came back to this project in January 2005. He did finally get his way, but not across the board. The most expensive scene of all was cut for the absurd reason that as it occurred quite early in the movie, nothing else later would match up to it. The scene involves the brothers' group being attacked by a tree. It made it to the dvd.

Generally the film was considered too dark a fantasy adventure for kids (maybe the torture chamber had something to do with that), and the many-times-reworked script was muddled. Undergoing problems with the Writers Guild of America, Gilliam and Tony Grisoni were not allowed to credit themselves as the writers of the screenplay, despite the many major tweaks they had made to Ehren Kruger's original script. (Kruger wrote *The Ring*, the Naomi Watts vehicle). Subversively they credited themselves as 'Dress Pattern Makers' and then told all who'd listen that the film was not necessarily made from a screenplay but 'from a dress pattern'.

The story plays fast and loose with the notion of the Grimm brothers as storytellers: they're characters rather than conceptualists here. They're a sort of nineteenth-century German ghostbusters. Variously portrayed as folk-lore collectors and con artists, Jacob Grimm, aka Jake (Ledger), and Wilhelm Grimm, aka Will (Damon), travel from village to village in the French-occupied Germany of 1811. They pretend to protect townsfolk from enchanted monsters and witches and to perform exorcisms. They're arrested by Cavaldi (Peter Stormare) and General Delatombe (Jonathan Pryce) in Marbaden. Young girls keep

TOP: Damon and Ledger at gunpoint
in *The Brothers Grimm*

ABOVE: Angelika, played by Lena Headey, helped
guide the brothers through a haunted forest

vanishing, possibly sacrifices. Local lovely Angelika (Lena Headey) guides them through a haunted forest. They're seriously tested when pitted against a real magical curse and have to find within themselves genuine courage for a shot at redemption. In a visually ravishing climax they face the evil Mirror Queen, played with relish by Monica Bellucci.

The catalogue of obstacles this movie had to overcome before completion earns some sympathy for Gilliam, the man behind such considerable efforts as the Monty Python films, *Brazil*, *Time Bandits*, *Fear and Loathing in Las Vegas*, *The Fisher King* and *Twelve Monkeys*. Originally cast were Nicole Kidman and Anthony Hopkins, but schedule problems then ruled them out. Robin Williams, likewise. Johnny Depp was rumoured to have been cast as Will. The cinematographer Nicola Percorini was axed by the Weinsteins. Gilliam and Matt Damon pushed for Samantha Morton to take the Lena

ABOVE: Confusingly, Heath had been cast as Will and Damon as Jake but they campaigned for a role reversal

Headey role, but the Weinsteins vetoed this. Even the music composer was changed late in the process, from Goran Bregovic to Dario Marianelli.

To top it all, Damon, who had, oddly, taken tango lessons as part of his preparation, and Ledger were cast the other way round – Damon as Jacob, Ledger as Will. They went on to petition for a character swap.

'It's not magic,' Will says of Jake's armour. 'It's just shiny.' After all the hassles, it's a wonder the film achieved the merit that it did. Although mightily confusing and uneven in tone, it is quite something to look at. Ledger's Jake is the romantic, innocent dreamer of the sibling pair; Damon's Will the pragmatic, cynical charmer. They work up a vague comedy double act.

Of Bellucci's imposing and durable Mirror Queen, Jake yells, 'She's still there, Will! She's still alive!'

LEFT: Naomi Watts accompanies Heath to the Screen Actors Guild Awards in Los Angeles in February 2004

ABOVE: Heath relaxing in Sydney with NfaMas of Melbourne hip-hop trio 1200 Techniques

'What, for five hundred years?' asks Will.

'Yeah,' answers Jake, 'but they haven't been kind, I can tell you that, Will.'

Another exchange sees Damon's Will announcing, 'You, my handsome friend, you have a heart.'

Ledger's Jake retorts, 'And you, Will, have enough bullshit to fill the Palace of Versailles.'

When the Grimm pair are happy (if philosophical), Jake praises their surname: 'It's a damn good name. Let's dance, come on!'

The Weinsteins flailed around trying to work out how to best promote the project. 'Eliminating Evil Since 1812' read one ad. Others rather weakly bleated, 'Fall under the Spell' and 'Once upon a time . . .' Another tried harder: 'No curse we can't reverse. No spell we can't break. No demon we can't exterminate.'

The New York Times sniffed at Damon's wig and prosthetic nose, adding that the film relied on too much 'shouting'. This was a criticism, surely, that could be levelled at most of today's blockbusters.

Total Film bemoaned the absence of Johnny Depp and reckoned that both Ledger and Damon, then prior to his *The Bourne Identity* reinvention, were 'miscast if affable'. It was 'a buddy movie with cut-and-paste witticisms', and

Ledger adopted 'a vaguely Northern accent'.

Time Out thought the pair 'bring emotional plausibility to the fraternal relationship, with its embedded jokes and frustrations, but offer little to root for.' Nearly all reviewers conceded that the final half-hour was gripping enough, thanks chiefly to 'Monica Belluci's fantastical radiance'.

Whatever the ups and downs of *The Brothers Grimm*, Heath Ledger must have greatly enjoyed the experience of working close to Terry Gilliam's inventive mind. He was, of course, to become involved in Gilliam's *The Imaginarium of Doctor Parnassus* in 2007 and early 2008. Tragically, he was to die before the film came anywhere close to completion. It was his final role.

Right now, however, despite the recent rollercoaster run of inconsistent movies, he was to accept the role that at last showed beyond all doubt what a talented actor he was. Heath had led the industry to expect the unexpected from him and his choice displayed all of his customary daring. It was a role that would change the public's perception of him, in a film that reverberated around the globe.

The role was Ennis Del Mar; the director was Ang Lee. The film was *Brokeback Mountain*, a very different kind of cowboy movie.

ABOVE: Heath and Jake Gyllenhaal took
on roles in *Brokeback Mountain* from which
many other actors had shied away

CHAPTER SEVEN

The Stillness of Him

'THE CHALLENGE WAS to capture the stillness of him,'
Heath Ledger said of Ennis Del Mar.
'I have a kind of semi-frantic, nervous energy. Harnessing that
was something I thought I'd have to work out. Shooting in the
wilderness, the stillness became almost an innate quality . . .'
Heath had long craved a taboo-breaking part that would allow
him to play against type. In *Brokeback Mountain*, which remains
the outstanding and definitive performance of his too-brief career,
he found it. The 2005 film which most critics believed deserved
to win the Best Film Oscar − equally, most thought Ledger should
have been honoured as Best Actor − became a huge talking point
across the world. It granted Ledger genuine superstar status and
unqualified industry respect. Based on an E. Annie Proulx short
story, its tale of two sixties ranch-hands, which swiftly became glibly
and reductively referred to as 'the gay cowboy movie', followed
Ledger's Ennis Del Mar and Jake Gyllenhaal's Jack Twist as
they struggled to come to terms with their sexuality over
decades of repression, angst and love.

ABOVE: *Brokeback Mountain* tells the story of a love affair between two ranch hands that spans twenty years

It begins in the summer of 1963 as a full-time ranch-hand (Ledger's Del Mar) and a jobbing rodeo cowboy (Gyllenhaal's Twist) take work herding sheep on *Brokeback Mountain*, a picturesque (fictional) range in Wyoming. The quiet, reticent Del Mar, whose parents are dead and who has been fending for himself from a young age, is nineteen and engaged. The more outgoing Twist has dreams of becoming a great rodeo rider. They endure a gruelling work load, facing hostile weather conditions, slim pickings and even animal attacks.

Their bond of friendship grows; they drink, they chat. Defying the orders of their crude boss Joe Aguirre (Randy Quaid) always to have one man guarding the sheep and one back at camp, one freezing cold night they share a tent. At first they huddle together just for warmth. The bolder of the two, Jack, initiates a physical relationship. Ennis is confused and hesitant until he finally engages with a vengeance. With nobody around for miles, a summer of the love that dared not speak its name ensues. Joe Aguirre cottons on, and is not impressed, while Ennis remains often in denial, but their attachment is sincere and strong.

When the summer ends, however, they separate and return to their contrasting lives. Ennis marries his betrothed,

Alma, played by his soon-to-be real-life partner, Michelle Williams. They hastily have two daughters.

Jack is less covert, allowing himself to be drawn to other men. Eventually, he meets feisty rodeo cowgirl Lureen Newsome – Anne Hathaway, playing against her formerly prim type. Her father is well-off thanks to a farm machinery sales business in Texas, and Lureen is keen for Jack to get involved, but he and her family don't click. Four years have now passed. Slightly bewildered, and nostalgic, Jack writes a letter to Ennis. Uncertain about his best course of action, Ennis makes up his mind to see Jack again, for once allowing his heart to rule his head.

Jack visits Ennis in Wyoming and their reunion is characterised by a passionate bear hug and more. Alma, scared, sees the intensity of their embrace. She is appalled, feeling as if a trapdoor has opened up under everything she thought she knew. Jack and Ennis, meanwhile, can't help themselves. They try to be discreet, going on 'fishing trips' together on the increasingly scenic *Brokeback Mountain*.

Jack would like things to be more fluid; Ennis urges caution and realism in homophobic times. Alma can stand it no more. She divorces Ennis, taking custody of their children.

ABOVE: *Rolling Stone* magazine said, 'Ledger's magnificent performance is an acting miracle.'

Hearing of the divorce, Jack rushes to Wyoming, hoping he and Ennis can now be free to be together full-time. Hearing Jack's romantic dreams, Ennis is appreciative but fearful, insisting that they'd be killed for being 'queer' if their secret came out. 'Bottom line is . . . we're around each other and . . . this thing, it grabs hold of us again . . . at the wrong place at the wrong time . . . and we're dead.' A childhood incident had scarred him for life.

The most he can agree to is quarterly visits from Jack, and quality private time spent around the mountains. For all these fleeting bursts of happiness and exhilaration, he is now struggling to make ends meet. Further along the road he gets together briefly with a waitress. He can't always get away from home to be with Jack, who travels to Mexico to try to assuage his urges, hoping to make Ennis jealous.

'Why is it always so friggin' cold?' Jack demands in one scene. 'We ought to go south where it's warm, you know. We ought to go to Mexico!'

'Mexico?' ponders Ennis. 'Hell, Jack, you know me. About all the travellin' I ever done is round a coffee pot lookin' for the handle . . .'

Then Ennis receives a postcard he'd sent to the thirty-nine-year-old Jack, returned with the word 'deceased' stamped across it. He contacts Lureen, Jack's wife, who tells him he was accidentally killed. The truth is worse: he was murdered for being 'queer', just as Ennis had dreaded. Lureen adds that Jack said he wanted his ashes spread at *Brokeback Mountain*, apparently a location which meant a lot to him. Ennis plucks up the courage to visit Jack's family and childhood home. Jack's father is adamant that the ashes will go to the family's conventional burial plot. His mother, however, invites Ennis to see Jack's old room. Here he finds two of their old shirts from '63, nestling together, still stained from a fight the two men once had. Ennis takes them with him when he goes.

Bereft, having lost everything, he moves into a small, depressing trailer. He drinks. His now-grown-up daughter, Alma Junior, visits, telling him she's getting married

and wants Ennis to attend the wedding. When she offers him furniture, he mumbles, 'Yeah, well . . . if you got nothin', you don't need nothin'.' She represents a younger generation, a fresher way of thinking and more reasonable approach to morals and personal choices. Ennis sits alone, beaten down by life, his heart broken. His proudest possessions are Jack's shirt and a picture postcard of the one place where he ever knew true happiness – *Brokeback Mountain*.

While, understandably, many focussed on Ang Lee's film's depiction of an area and era in which homophobia was the norm and where homosexual love was repressed through self-preservation instincts, as well as recognising his subversive reinvention of the definitively American, traditionally 'macho' Western genre, what made the film transcend its 'messages' was its deeply moving encapsulation of the joys and pains of love, regardless of gender or age. Every love is unique, it seemed to say. It studied the irrational forces which drive two people towards each other and the society which often tries to keep them apart.

ABOVE: Heath 'marrying' his future partner Michelle Williams
as Ennis and Alma in *Brokeback Mountain*

It looked at lies, at denial ('You know I ain't queer', 'Me neither'), at self-expression. It questioned responsibility, duty, stereotyping and consequences, but above all it was a love story, filmed with magnificent aplomb and acted with a wonderful restraint which emphasised the under-currents of emotion.

Ledger's performance was for the main part internalised, subtly powerful. Although the film earned a big audience, and the awards and accolades came teeming down, he and Gyllenhaal had taken a risk in taking these roles. Ledger may have played a gay character long ago in *Sweat*, but this was a much grander stage. Several big-name actors had decided against participating in the movie. Ledger was persuaded by three chief factors. His desire to tackle far-from-obvious roles was one. His then girlfriend, Naomi Watts, had also encouraged him to go for it.

Then there was a factor from Heath's own past: his uncle, Neil Bell, when aged twenty, had been told by his father that as he was gay he was 'ill', and must either go to hospital or leave town. He left Perth, moved to Los Angeles,

and underwent years of extreme denial, acting macho by participating in bare knuckle boxing in the Nevada desert, and other such endeavours.

There are countless perfectly-gauged scenes in *Brokeback Mountain*, and Ledger and Gyllenhaal approach them with exquisite judgment. Under pressure, Ennis says, 'I'm going to tell you this one time, Jack Twist, and I ain't foolin'. What I don't know – all them things I don't know – could get you killed if I come to know them. I ain't jokin'.'

'Tell you what,' cries Jack. 'We coulda had a good life together . . . had a place of our own. But you didn't want it, Ennis! So what we got now is *Brokeback Mountain*. Everything's built on that. That's all we got, boy . . . I wish I knew how to quit you . . .'

As their first summer together ends, it is what isn't said that stings. Jack ventures: 'You gonna do this again next summer?'

'Well, maybe not,' mutters Ennis. 'Like I said, Alma and me's gettin' married in November, so . . . I'll try and get something on a ranch, I guess. And you?'

LEFT: 'You know, friend, this is a goddamn bitch of an unsatisfactory situation.'

'I might go up to my Daddy's place and give him a hand through the winter,' sighs Jack. 'But I might be back . . . if the army don't get me.'

Casually, Ennis says, 'Well . . . I guess I'll see you around, huh?'

After a long pause, the stunned Jack says, 'Right.'

So much they want to say but dare not.

Jack expresses it best when he muses, 'Brokeback got us good, don't it?'

It's Ennis who is less cavalier, more timid, at least in public. 'You ever get the feelin' . . . I don't know . . . when you're in town and someone looks at you all suspicious, like he knows? And then you go out on the pavement and everyone looks like they know, too?'

Jack suggests he moves out, comes to 'some place different', like Texas.

'Texas?' splutters Ennis. 'Sure, maybe you can convince Alma to let you and Lureen adopt the girls. And we can just live together herding sheep. And it'll rain money . . . and whiskey will flow in the streams – Jack, that's real smart.'

'Go to hell, Ennis,' retorts the harmonica-playing Jack. 'If you wanna live your miserable life, then go right ahead . . . I was just thinking' out loud.'

'Yep, you're a real thinker there. Goddamn. Jack Twist. Got it all figured out, ain't ya?'

Such arguments are telling, but the poignancy of their situation is also well evoked when Ennis tries to placate Jack, at least as best he can.

'We can get together . . . once in a while, way the hell out in the middle of nowhere, but . . .'

'Once in a while?' exclaims Jack. 'Every four years?'

'If you can't fix it, Jack, you gotta stand it.'

'For how long?'

'For as long as we can ride it. There ain't no reins on this one.'

On another occasion Ennis gives much away. 'Speak for yourself,' he tells Jack. 'You may be a sinner, but I ain't yet had the opportunity.'

In another scene Jack says, 'There ain't never enough time, never enough . . .' Another great line he offers is, 'You know, friend, this is a goddam bitch of an unsatisfactory situation.'

To the immense satisfaction of everybody involved in this groundbreaking film, the screenplay of which had been penned by Larry McMurtry and Diana Ossana as far back as 1997, the reviews (if you discount the conservative Christian right) were euphoric, the subsequent awards plentiful. 'Love is a force of nature' stated the tag-line, and so, it appeared, was the film. *The Observer* praised 'two excellent, complementary performances' while *The Guardian*

RIGHT: Ennis and Alma were to have two daughters, while Heath and Michelle would have one of their own

acclaimed 'a genuine masterpiece . . . beautifully composed and wonderfully acted.' *Variety* hailed Heath: 'Ledger is powerfully impressive as a frightened, limited man ill-equipped to deal with what life throws at him. Mumbling, looking down, Ennis at times looks as though he's going to explode from his inchoate feelings. This is . . . a dazzling year for Ledger.'

Meanwhile *Total Film* called him 'a tragic hero of real stature, his rugged veneer slowly crumbling to show a broken man who recognises too late his last chance of happiness.'

One of the most glowing and astute reviews of all came from *Rolling Stone*'s Peter Travers. 'Ennis lives in fear of coming out – he relates a harrowing childhood incident in which he saw a man tortured and killed for the crime of living with another man. And so he forbids himself happiness with the one person he has ever truly loved. Ledger's magnificent performance is an acting miracle. He seems to tear it from his insides. Ledger doesn't just know how Ennis moves, speaks and listens: he knows how he breathes. To see him inhale the scent of a shirt hanging in Jack's closet is to take measure of the pain of love lost . . .'

Behind the scenes, there had been much turmoil in bringing such a seemingly controversial major film together. Gus Van Sant and Joel Schumacher had both been interested in directing before Lee, the chameleon behind *Sense and Sensibility* and *Crouching Tiger, Hidden Dragon* as well as *The Hulk* and *Lust, Caution*, had taken over. Actress Emma Thompson had once revealed that after trouble with sheep on the set of *Sense and Sensibility*, Lee had sworn to her that he'd never work with sheep again. Then he took on a movie that involved sheep-herding.

Boogie Nights star Mark Wahlberg told *Premiere* magazine that at one point, he and Joaquin Phoenix (*Gladiator, Walk the Line*) were considered for the lead roles. He added that, although he mulled it over because of his 'brother-like' relationship with Phoenix, some scenes were ultimately too sexually graphic for him.

Sienna Miller (*Factory Girl, Interview*, soon to co-star with Ledger in *Casanova*) had auditioned for the Lureen role taken by Anne Hathaway. Hathaway in turn had introduced herself to Ang Lee as a little-known Broadway actress, keeping her more twee and innocent work in the movies *The Princess Diaries* and *Ella Enchanted* secret from him. Fortunately for her, he had no idea that she had been in two such highly commercially successful films, and thought he was giving her her big break.

Lee had intended to cut any frontal nudity out of the film, but after paparazzi snapped Ledger and a stunt double for Gyllenhaal jumping naked off a rock into a lake and the

ABOVE: Heath celebrating with Jack Gyllenhaal at the Toronto Film Festival *Brokeback Mountain* part in September 2005

RIGHT: Heath and Gyllenhaal supporting Ang Lee at the Directors Guild of America Awards in Los Angeles in January 2006

subsequent shots appeared on the internet, Lee and Ledger shrugged and placed the scene in the European version of *Brokeback*, if not the American one. In another amusing accident, it was reported that Ledger, in character, once kissed Gyllenhaal so vigorously that he almost broke his nose. Ledger also told *The Philadelphia Enquirer* that an extra sequence was shot that was discarded because all involved felt it didn't work. In this Ennis and Jack assisted some sixties hippies whose car had swerved into the river. The scene – not evident in the original short story and probably an attempt to shore up the cowboys' 'good guy' qualities – took a week of shooting, but was deemed to sit awkwardly with the general overall tone of the movie.

Prior to principal photography, Lee had given Ledger and Gyllenhaal copies of the book *Farm Boys: Lives of the Gay Men from the Rural Midwest* by Will Fellows, feeling it might help them in grasping their characters. Gyllenhaal, however, emphasised that Ennis and Jack 'probably don't even know what "gay" means.' And after completion of the film, *Brokeback* author E. Annie Proulx (the story first appeared in the *New Yorker* in 1997) gifted both actors an autographed copy of her original. Gyllenhaal's was signed 'to Jake', but she mistakenly signed Ledger's 'to Ennis'. Realising her error, she set off for a private preview screening of the movie in Hollywood emerging to state that Ledger 'really was Ennis', and leaving her inscription intact. She declared that

LEFT: Heath and Michelle together at the *Brokeback Mountain*
New York premiere in December 2005

ABOVE: Together with Matt Damon at the Venice Film Festival
promoting *The Brothers Grimm* in September 2005

Ledger had embodied Ennis 'in every way that I wrote him.'

He was undoubtedly a major factor in the film's success. 'The film is Ennis' tragedy,' wrote *Time Out*. 'It becomes painfully obvious that he left his soul on *Brokeback Mountain*. It's a tough act to witness and one that Ledger handles superbly, delivering an increasingly sad, mumbling and desperate performance streaked with loneliness and alienation . . . this is Hollywood's first bona fide, well made and commercially viable gay weepie.' In its first week on release, opening in just five American cinemas, it broke the record for the highest per-screen gross takings of any non-animated movie in history. Producer James Schamus announced that even in this first week of limited release, it

had recouped its cost, so economically had it been made.

For Ang Lee, there was a downside: China, considering homosexuality thoroughly taboo, banned the movie. There were also some protests and grumbles in the more reactionary territories of America. Most of the rest of the world, however, embraced it. At the 2005 Venice Film Festival, Ledger starred in no less than three major films, *Brokeback Mountain*, *The Brothers Grimm* and *Casanova*. As for awards, he needed a bigger trophy cabinet.

Heath received Best Actor awards from the Australian Film Institute, the Ohio Film Critics Circle, and establishments as far-flung as San Francisco, New York, Las Vegas and Phoenix. Nominations poured in at the Oscars,

LEFT: Michelle was pregnant with Matilda Rose at the Los Angeles premiere of *The Brothers Grimm* in August 2005

ABOVE: Michelle and Heath at the Gotham Awards in New York in November 2005, one month after Matilda was born

the Golden Globes, the Baftas, the Screen Actors Guild Awards and the Independent Spirit Awards. Inevitably, there was a Best Kiss award to Ledger and Gyllenhaal from the MTV Movie Awards.

While Ang Lee won an Oscar and a Golden Globe, the film – the bookies' hot favourite on the night – was pipped to the Best Film Oscar at the eleventh hour by Paul Haggis' *Crash*. It did win the Golden Globe, and Oscars were bagged for music and best adapted screenplay. Ledger, however, expected by many to win the Oscar in a healthily competitive field, had to smile politely and applaud while Philip Seymour Hoffman took the prize for his role as Truman Capote in *Capote*. Gyllenhaal, nominated as Best

Supporting Actor, ceded to George Clooney in *Syriana* (although he did win a Bafta), while Michelle Williams, nominated as Best Supporting Actress, saw Rachel Weisz win for her role in *The Constant Gardener*.

Ledger did not leave *Brokeback Mountain* empty-handed. He won great kudos for his brave performance in a fine film, and the respect of his acting peers that he had so long desired. And in Michelle Williams, he met his new partner and the mother of his only child. 'She's my soul mate and we couldn't love each other any more than we do already,' he said, happily. 'We're like two peas in a pod.'

CHAPTER EIGHT

Michelle and Matilda

BORN ON 9 SEPTEMBER 1980 in a small Montana town named Kalispell, Michelle Williams was to become a thoroughly unconventional young woman. Her father, Larry, a commodities trader and once a Republican Party candidate for the Montana State senate, became divorced from her mother Carla. More unusually, Williams, at age fifteen, 'legally and financially emancipated' herself from her parents. 'We were living in San Diego at that point,' she told *Wonderland* magazine. 'Other kids around me were going to Los Angeles for auditions. The idea was that I could get more and better jobs if I became emancipated because then you don't need a social worker and you can work longer hours. My dad is very work-oriented and I think I picked up on that.' She later conceded, 'As a parent myself now, it's hard for me to understand.'

LEFT: Heath and Michelle attending the
Vanity Fair Oscars party in LA in 2006

She wouldn't let her own daughter do it. 'I've always been very strong-willed. It served me well.' At sixteen she won the Robbins Trading Company World Cup Championship of Futures Trading by turning $10,000 into $100,000 – the second highest profit in the tournament's history. She has a younger sister, Paige, and three older half-siblings (Jason, Kelley and Sara) from her father's first marriage.

She won small TV and film parts after attending Santa Fe Christian High School from where she graduated aged fifteen. There was her alien in *Species* and her part with Jessica Lange in *A Thousand Acres*. The young actress, an avid reader, broke through from 1998 onwards in TV hit *Dawson's Creek*, alongside Mrs Cruise-in-waiting, Katie Holmes. Here Williams played 'bad girl' Jen Lindley. She was chosen as one of *Teen People Magazine*'s '21 Hottest Stars Under 21' in 1999, and was on *Entertainment Weekly*'s annual 'It List' the following year. She stripped naked in an off-Broadway play, *Killer Joe*. 'That was probably a reaction to *Dawson's Creek*.'

Her face established, she now found those 'more and better jobs' flying in. The quality varied from *Halloween: H20* to *Dick*, opposite Kirsten Dunst, and *But I'm a Cheerleader*. Of her 1995 film, *Timemaster*, she famously said, 'It was so awful. We turned the "M" upside down and called it *Timewaster*.'

An acclaimed turn in *If These Walls Could Talk* 2 led to Williams being cast with Christina Ricci (her then room-mate: 'We were wild,' said Williams) in 2001's *Prozac Nation*, and the underrated British film *Me Without You*, with Anna Friel, in which Williams managed a decent British accent. There followed *The Station Agent*, *Imaginary Heroes* and the role of Samantha in Ethan Hawke's *The Hottest State*, based on his own novel. In 2003 *ELLE girl* placed her among their '25 Favourite Hot, Young, Talented New Stars'. Not everything went like clockwork though: she said in one interview, 'Outside of the business during a dry spell, I once scooped ice cream at a country fair, and I ate more than I sold.

Making a cone is difficult, and I lost so many scoops into the chocolate swirl . . .'

On the road to fame Williams wrote and sold a screenplay, *Blink*, yet to be filmed. She dated Conor Oberst, a recording star under the name Bright Eyes, who wrote songs about her. Another boyfriend was Andy Herod, singer/songwriter with the band The Comas, whom she dated for two years. His album *Conductor* is reputedly about their relationship and his subsequent broken heart. Williams features in the short film of the same name made to accompany the record. Among her collection of rare books is a first edition of F. Scott Fitzgerald's *The Great Gatsby*.

It was *Brokeback Mountain,* however, which brought her recognition beyond teen and indie circles. As Alma, Ennis' wife, she dovetailed brilliantly with Heath Ledger, and was, like him, Oscar-nominated. Not that this overly boosted her confidence: 'I can't watch myself in movies,' she said. 'I used to think I was cool. Now, my standpoint is that I can't be fair. So I can't pass any judgment.'

What, presumably, did boost her confidence was that she and Ledger became a real-life couple. They were soon engaged, and she gave birth to a baby girl, Matilda Rose, on 28 October 2005, in Brooklyn. Matilda Rose Ledger – a highly Australian-sounding name – weighed six pounds and five ounces. The godparents were *Brokeback* co-star Jake Gyllenhaal and Williams' former *Dawson's Creek* colleague Busy Philipps.

When Michelle's former headmaster expressed distasteful homophobic views about *Brokeback Mountain* in the press, Michelle was '. . . disappointed. It never bothered me what he says, I never liked him anyway. There are always going to be people with contrary opinions, but I'm awfully proud of the film.'

The new Ledger-Williams family were blissfully happy at first. Heath enjoyed living in Brooklyn, although early in their relationship the couple had used the Chateau

Marmont hotel in Hollywood as their West Coast base. 'Brooklyn seems to me the closest thing in America to Europe,' he said. 'The neighbours and locals are beautiful people. It's like a village.' Neighbours in the Boerum Hill area spoke of a 'laid-back mom' who enjoyed children's parties and opened her house to Halloween trick-or-treaters. 'Michelle and Matilda gave out good candy together,' recalled one local dad.

Love was assuredly in the air. Heath gushed about the experience of parenthood. 'Matilda is adorable, and beautifully observant and wise. Michelle and I love her so much. Becoming a father exceeds all my expectations. It's the most remarkable experience I've ever had – it's marvellous.'

'She looks just like her father,' was to become a frequent comment from friends and family. Domesticity's routines also seemed to agree with Ledger. He later told one interviewer, 'My life right now is, I wouldn't say reduced to food, but my duties in life are that I wake up, cook breakfast, clean the dishes, prepare lunch, clean those dishes, go to the market, get fresh produce, cook dinner, clean those dishes and then sleep if I can. And I love it. I actually adore it.'

The mention of problems with sleeping was, however, with hindsight, ominous. The other worm in the apple of their contentment was that, as a celebrity couple, they were constantly being bothered by the media and paparazzi. Back in 2001, Heath, talking to the *National Post*, had tried to wax philosophical about the problem. 'Most of the time you don't even know they're there. Now, that's the scary thing. It's really strange and invading, but I'm still working it all out. I try to not let it bother me. I really try and find the humour in all of it. And if I want to swim naked in my pool, I'm still going to do it. I certainly don't want to feel that I have to change everything in my life that I do just to cater to them. I just won't let that happen.'

Yet, with the wave of added fame and – given its subject matter – notoriety that *Brokeback Mountain* brought in some quarters, the hysterical media shifted their attention on Ledger and Williams up a gear. He was now one of the most recognisable faces in movies. In the warped logic of these circles, the couple were seen as fair game. There was a furore when, dogged by persistent paparazzi, Ledger was accused of assaulting a photographer in Sydney, and of spitting at him. The ever-so-noble paparazzi thought

they were getting their own back when they squirted water pistols at Heath and Michelle as they took to the red carpet at the Sydney premiere of *Brokeback Mountain*, spoiling what should have been a proud moment for the actor in his home country. The pressure of celebrity, and of work's conflicting schedules, ultimately split Ledger and Williams apart in 2007 as Heath wrestled with his role in *I'm Not There*. The celebrity/media-hounding factor may even have played a part in Heath's sad demise.

After the separation, the two shared custody, employing a nanny, but Brooklyn-ites continued to describe Michelle as a 'hands-on' mother. 'Matilda never seems to want to leave her side,' noted another neighbour.

While things were good, Michelle, voted among *People* magazine's '100 Most Beautiful People in 2007', was still winning promising roles. Of course, the couple both featured in Todd Haynes' Bob Dylan reverie *I'm Not There* (she as Coco Rivington), and 'in the can' she has Spike Jonze's *Synecdoche, New York* with Philip Seymour Hoffman, who pipped Ledger to the Oscar, and Catherine Keener. There is also *Incendiary*, with Ewan McGregor, and *The Tourist*, again with McGregor. She was shooting *Blue*

Valentine, with Ryan Gosling, when news of Heath's death came through. Filming was suspended indefinitely. Also on hold is *Mammoth*, by Swedish director Lukas Moodysson, wherein she was playing a New York City trauma surgeon, a role she prepared for by trailing a doctor for months. 'I thought: I've missed my calling,' she said. 'The sense of purpose made me wish I'd become a doctor.'

Asked by *Wonderland* magazine shortly before Heath's death whether she was recognised on the street in New York, she replied, 'It depends. It's quietened down . . . When you're in a relationship with somebody who is also a public personality then it doubles the attention from the media. When you minus that equation it's just less enticing. That's been the bonus, the plus side of the break-up for me. It was so pervading, it got bad there for a while. Every time I walk out the door I still worry. I'm not good at that stuff. It really used to affect me.'

Tragically, in January 2008 she was to find herself the centre of media attention all over again, for reasons that had no plus side.

CHAPTER NINE

Deep In The Character's Skin

THESE WERE PROVING to be Heath Ledger's golden years.
His maverick tendencies strengthened. The acclaim for
Brokeback Mountain ringing in his ears, he elected to follow it with
a role so extremely different that you wonder if his advisers were
over-compensating. Where do you go after you've played a
'gay cowboy'? Naturally, you play *Casanova*, the poster boy for
every heterosexual serial seducer in history.
Lasse Hallstrom's glossy take on the libidinous legend was an
energetic, wilfully over-the-top, patchy romp, perhaps unsure
if it wanted to be farce or fantasy. Its sources of inspiration
seemed to be *The Three Musketeers* and various *Zorro* flicks.
Ledger, as ever, gave it his all.

LEFT: Heath in flamboyant attire
for his portrayal of Casanova

ABOVE: Heath and Sienna Miller share a tender
moment in a scene from *Casanova*

Having run into trouble philandering in gloriously
photogenic old Venice, circa 1753, Casanova is advised
to restore his reputation by marrying a woman of spotless
virtue. Instead, he's attracted to Sienna Miller's Francesca
Bruni, a swashbuckling, ahead-of-her-time feminist
who thinks his bedroom larks are deeply shameful. So,
shoehorning in a Shakespearean twist, Casanova adopts
a series of disguises and strives to lure her away from her
rich and portly fiancé Paprizzio, played by Oliver Platt.
Cue mistaken identities and dramatically convenient
misunderstandings. At the same time, our man must steer
clear of a stream of smitten females and Jeremy Irons' severe
inquisitor Pucci, who seeks to make a moral example of this
prototype bad boy. Lena Olin, Omid Djalili, Ken Stott and
Helen McCrory also feature, as well as *Quadrophenia* and
Mike Leigh veteran Phil Davis.

   Scripted in curious fashion by Jeffrey Hatcher and
Kimberley Simi, it's as if the film bemuses Hallstrom, who'd
made his name with the likes of *The Cider House Rules*, *What's
Eating Gilbert Grape*, *The Shipping News* and *Chocolat*. Maybe a
director with a darker vision would have been better suited
to the project. If, however, you go along with its happy-
go-lucky, tongue-in-cheek feel, it has its buoyant spells,
mostly involving chases and swordplay. 'Plenty of good
ingredients,' remarked one reviewer, 'but the result is raw,
or at best half-baked.' One assumes Ledger's army of female
admirers enjoyed the results most. 'Ledger's charisma
and intelligence,' *Time Out* noted, 'deserve better than this
cornily conceived, hamfistedly executed doodle on baroque
themes . . .' The goodwill Ledger earned through *Brokeback
Mountain* meant that he emerged blameless from the affair.
The casting must have made fine sense on paper. For some,
it hit the spot. Praising a 'fluffy, frivolous, wholly enjoyable'
film, Salon.com commented on 'Ledger's low-key wit and
flowing tresses' and the 'mischievous glint in his eye.'

   Less populist and of a much more challenging nature
was a low-budget Australian film which had been in the
can a while and now gained a more prominent release
thanks to Ledger's renown and status. *Candy* premiered at
the 2006 Berlin Film Festival. A 'bohemian junkies in love'
tale of the ilk of Darren Aronovsky's *Requiem for a Dream* or
another undervalued Aussie film of the time, *Little Fish* (in
which Ledger's friends and compatriots Martin Henderson
and Cate Blanchett starred), this was helmed by director

ABOVE: Sienna Miller played a swashbuckling feminist who was, ultimately, won over by Casanova

Neil Armfield. The title referred to both the lead female character and a certain drug. Abbie Cornish, discovered in the movie *Somersault*, played Candy, an art student/painter, while Ledger – taking one of the riskier roles he preferred – played Dan, a would-be poet who falls in love with her.

'The future was a thing that gleamed. The present was so very, very good,' intones Dan, at first a cocky narrator, later a sad, desperate mess looking for a vein to inject. Dan degenerates under the narcotics' influence to a shambling, prideless scamster, while Candy slides into prostitution and insanity. 'The world is very bewildering to a junkie.' Egged on to heroin addiction by professor and smackhead Casper (Geoffrey Rush, another Australian acting giant, at his seedy best), the couple distressingly spiral downwards, hooked on each other but mostly on the wrong stuff. They shunt from Sydney to Melbourne in an effort to get clean. They fail. 'We had a lot going for us,' intones the self-deluding Dan. 'In the perfect place, where the noise did not intrude, our world was so very complete . . .'

Despite over-obvious chapter headings (Heaven, Earth, Hell), Armfield's harrowing film remained resolutely non-judgmental and, for the most part, avoided the pitfalls of

cliché. Ledger, Cornish and Rush were all nominated for awards by the Australian Film Institute. 'An excellent, heartfelt film,' thought *The Guardian*'s Peter Bradshaw. 'Cornish and Ledger give performances of absolute conviction . . . an inexpressibly painful study of a young couple whose love is consecrated to heroin.' *In Film Australia* was even more enthusiastic. 'Heath Ledger's Dan is one of the most truthful portrayals of his many-varied and talented career. That he's playing a gritty contemporary urban fringe character for once, following his dashing romantic role as Casanova, is refreshing, and reminds us of his stunning performance in 1999's *Two Hands*.' It also showed that Ledger, despite innumerable big-money offers, remained keen to support the Australian film industry which had granted him his first real shot. 'Ledger plays the part of the scheming user exceptionally well,' agreed the *New York Times*. 'He's deep in the character's skin right from the start.' It added that he appeared to benefit from speaking in his native accent, as opposed to the 'clenched jaw' he tends to adopt for an American one.

'People just love to bash LA,' Ledger had said, innocently, back in 2000, as he found his feet both in

LEFT: *Casanova* was a happy-go-lucky
romp played as a farce

ABOVE: *Candy* gave Heath the opportunity to take on a
role with the sort of intensity in which he revelled

America and as an actor. 'People say it's so pretentious, so arrogant, so this and that. But it's truly a wonderful place. You don't have to go to the places where that stuff goes on. You don't have to go to Beverly Hills, you don't have to go to the parties. You can live up in the Lower Canyon and live such a perfectly healthy, beautiful, fun life with all your friends. You can drive two hours one way and be at the Joshua Tree desert, two hours another way you're skiing at Big Bear. Sure, it can get full-on and that's why it's good to get out. But it's too easy just to say, "Nope, I hate it. I'm not living there anymore."' Ultimately, of course, Heath was to base himself in New York, not LA.

While it can be glib to read too many parallels into the life-imitating-art equation, *Candy* is a film whose subject matter may draw people to look at it again in the wake of Heath's tragic medication-induced death. It had been filmed before *Brokeback* but, released later, pulled a bigger audience than it might otherwise have done. Heath had found a new extra-curricular activity, too. He co-founded

the record label Music Masses Co with good friend Ben Harper, a well-known singer and musician, and directed Harper's video for the song 'Morning Yearning', as well as videos for Aussie act N'Fa.

As Heath, always shy, tussled with his next role as a symbolic incarnation of Bob Dylan in *I'm Not There*, he found himself so wound up and stressed that he increased his intake of pills, confessing that sometimes he slept as little as two hours a night. He split with Michelle in September of 2007. *I'm Not There*, released just before Christmas of that year, was to be the last film in which they'd appear together. It was also to be the last Heath Ledger film released in his lifetime.

In 1965, Bob Dylan, reading an article about himself, muttered, 'God, I'm glad I'm not me.' Finding himself increasingly fascinated by Dylan thirty-five years later, Todd Haynes was spending time in Portland, Oregon. He was distracted from writing the Oscar-nominated screenplay of *Far From Heaven* by visions of Dylan, and wondered how he could capture his mysteries on film. 'I found myself curiously

ABOVE: Abbie Cornish starred as Candy alongside
Heath in the tale of two ill-fated lovers

coming back to him at a moment in my life where I was
looking for change.' As Haynes delved into biographies
of the singer, he 'kept confronting this theme of him as an
artist unnerving his following again and again by changing
who he was – sometimes to such a degree that the people
around him described it as literally shape-shifting in front of
their eyes.'

Such a statement calls to mind some of the better actors.
Certainly this project was to present another opportunity for
Heath Ledger to offer us another facet of himself, another
perspective on and glimpse into his now troubled soul.

'I wanted,' continued Haynes, 'to have the film be
composed of different actors in completely different stories
and genres, each one based on the musical themes and
characteristics of a particular period in Dylan's life.' The
director had attempted something similar with regard to
the personae of David Bowie and Iggy Pop in his earlier,
spectacularly under-rated movie *Velvet Goldmine*. He'd also
revealed his near-obsession with singers in *Superstar: The Karen*

Carpenter Story, where he'd used Barbie dolls as his 'cast'.

Haynes piqued the interest of Dylan's manager, Jeff
Rosen, and soon learned that Dylan approved of the
concept in principle. Knuckling down to pen the script with
Oren Moverman, Haynes was encouraged by Rosen to give
his own 'weird interpretation'. Thus, in the provocative
and imaginative *I'm Not There*, several actors play differing
personas of Dylan in an enigmatic, episodic movie. 'Some
correspond to a recognisable period and look . . . others are
more metaphorical, blending influences and passions and
imagery that extend over his entire career . . .'

The Dylans are Woody the folk singer (played by Marcus
Carl Franklin), protest singer Jack Rollins (played by Christian
Bale, also star of *Velvet Goldmine*), Arthur the Rimbaud-
influenced poet (Ben Whishaw), Jude the electric-guitar rebel
(an Oscar-nominated Cate Blanchett), and the Billy the Kid
cypher (Richard Gere). And then there's Robbie.

Robbie – Heath Ledger – dominates the sections which
focus on Dylan's personal life and the love affair which fuels

ABOVE: The relationship between Dan and Candy descended into a drugs-induced hell

ABOVE: Heath and Abbie Cornish were both nominated for Australian Film Institute awards for *Candy*

many of his most telling songs. During the Vietnam War era, Robbie is an arrogant, womanising counter-culture actor (we see him participate in a film within the film) who is in a relationship with the painter Claire (Charlotte Gainsbourg). He's hyped as the next James Dean.

In fact, in the 1965 film within the film, *Grains of Sand*, he's playing the vanished Jack Rollins, hammily bawling lines like, 'I was only a pawn in their game!' As years pass his time spent away and neglect, bordering on contempt, towards Claire gradually erode their mutual respect. This loosely sets out to mirror Dylan's romances with Sara Lownds and Suze Rotolo.

It starts well, like most romances. When Robbie and Claire first get together they make love to the strains of Dylan's 'I Want You', and head to the country to pick up his motorcycle. They're soon married with two kids. Later, there is marital war and the battle for custody of their two children. It's unnerving to think that Ledger's relationship with Michelle Williams was suffering at the same time.

Heath invariably spoke of daughter Matilda with great love. 'Fatherhood has changed me, I feel things on a different level . . . she is the most beautiful, beautiful girl. Being away from her, it's kind of like your whole body has a lump in its throat.' Matilda's mother, of course, also features briefly in the film, playing a blonde Edie Sedgwick type called Coco Rivington pursued, futilely, by Jude (that is, Blanchett as Dylan).

Robbie is arguably the least flattering aspect of Dylan presented in *I'm Not There*, a warts and all portrait. 'We all know he's brilliant,' said Haynes, acknowledging the influence of Jean-Luc Godard on this depiction. 'I didn't

need to paint a puff piece of him. I thought that the conflicts and contradictions of his personality were more interesting than just patting him on the back. What was remarkable was how Dylan's management allowed me to do that!'

Also remarkable is Ledger's performance, one which, by his own admission, he truly anguished over.

'It's not about me any more,' cries Robbie, looking up at a billboard of Jack Rollins. 'It's all about him.'

Later, when Claire asks him what is 'at the centre of your world,' the moody, sullen Robbie snaps, 'Well, I'm twenty-two. I guess I would say . . . me.'

Again, Haynes' comments on Dylan could apply equally to the actor. 'Freedom is not just about finding out who you really are and staying there. There maybe is no such thing. True freedom is the ability to, the necessity even, to reinvent yourself. The minute you try to grab hold of him, he's no longer there. He's like a flame – if you try to hold him in your hand you'll surely get burned . . .'

In *Uncut* magazine, Allan Jones hailed 'an audaciously prismatic portrait, as contrary, confrontational, playful, unpredictable, allusive and often just as downright funny as its subject.' At the London Film Festival it was pitched as 'inspired . . . rooted in real depth of knowledge . . . with tremendous leads.' Although Cate Blanchett deservedly stole most of the acting plaudits here, Ledger drew praise from *Total Film* ('outstanding'), and from *Rolling Stone* for 'digging deep into a challenging role.'

Perhaps only Heath himself knew exactly how deep. Todd Haynes, who had become a close friend, was among those who spoke at his memorial service in California.

ABOVE: Heath enjoying himself at a press conference
for *Candy* in Berlin in February 2006

CHAPTER TEN

Accidental Death

AND SUDDENLY, Heath wasn't there.
On the afternoon of 22 January 2008, he was found
face down, unconscious and naked on the bed in his
Soho, Manhattan, apartment at 421 Broome Street. His
housekeeper discovered him, having gone to inform him of
the arrival of a masseuse he'd booked for an appointment.
She called the emergency services. The Police Department
announced that Heath was declared dead by medics at
3.30 p.m. Traces of six different prescription drugs were
found in his body. No illegal drugs were discovered.
The worldwide media huffed and puffed, flinging out all
manner of tangential stories, including a red herring that
the apartment belonged to actress Mary-Kate Olsen,
a claim promptly denied by Olsen's publicist. Rumour
and counter-rumour thrived, implying a suicide.

ABOVE: Heath as Robbie with Charlotte
Gainsbourg in *I'm Not There*

The breaking story of Ledger's death exploded chaotically across the Internet, with errors, inconsistencies and confusion flying around. 'In the new digital media's race to break stories in minutes, accuracy has been left in the dust,' noted one expert. 'While, in the past, journalists had hours to vet and craft a story, reporting now often unfolds in real time.'

Dying aged just twenty-eight, Ledger became a tragic figure, potentially a James Dean for a younger generation. A distraught Michelle Williams issued her statement. A spokeswoman gave the technically correct cause of death: 'acute intoxication by the combined effects of oxycodone, hydrocodone, diazepam, alprazolam and doxylamine.' Some of these are more commonly known as the anti-anxiety medications Valium and the sleeping aids Restoril and Unisom. Ledger's father, Kim, added later: 'While no medications were taken in excess, we learned today the combination of doctor-prescribed drugs proved lethal for our boy. Heath's accidental death serves as a caution to the hidden dangers of combining prescription medication, even at low dosage.'

Heath's words to the *New York Times* the previous year were recalled. 'Last week I probably slept an average of two hours a night. I couldn't stop thinking. My body was exhausted, and my mind was still going.' He'd hinted that his work on the new Batman film *The Dark Knight* and on *I'm Not There* had exacerbated his condition. The workload had not eased up. Just two days prior to his death he'd been in London, where he'd been filming Terry Gilliam's *The Imaginarium of Doctor Parnassus*. The production was about to move to Vancouver.

Heath's parents returned to Perth the following week, Michelle accompanying them, to prepare for the funeral. They planned to lay the body to rest in the family plot. They issued another dignified statement. 'We remain humble as parents and a family, among millions of parents worldwide who may have suffered the tragic loss of a child,' it read. 'Few can understand the hollow, wrenching, and enduring agony parents silently suffer when a child predeceases them. Today's results put an end to speculation, but our son's beautiful spirit and enduring memory will remain forever in our hearts.'

On the Sunday, 2 February, there had been a memorial service in Los Angeles, at the Sony lot in Culver City. Michelle and Matilda were joined by friends Tom Cruise and Katie Holmes, Ledger's ex Naomi Watts, *I'm Not There* director Todd Haynes (who gave a few words), and Heath's good friend Ben Harper, who sang. Also present were actors

ABOVE: A contemplative pose as the troubled Robbie in *I'm Not There*

ABOVE: Heath in a light-hearted mood promoting *I'm Not There* at the Venice Film Festival in September 2007

Josh Hartnett, who said, 'It's a horrible, horrible loss. He was a great guy,' and Emile Hirsch. A specially prepared slideshow moved guests to tears. One described it as 'a beautiful, moving celebration of his life.' Williams' mother, Carla, and Matilda's godparents, Busy Philipps and Jake Gyllenhaal, had also rushed to support Michelle.

Afterwards, Michelle gathered a small group of close friends at her base in the Chateau Marmont to further remember the father of her child. His *Casanova* co-star, Sienna Miller, and her boyfriend, Rhys Ifans, were among them. One told *Us* magazine, 'Michelle sat and told stories about Heath for several hours over dinner. Everybody was comforting her. It was very sombre.'

The film she'd been working on herself at the time, *Blue Valentine*, was put on hold. 'She was always really vulnerable,

so this has shaken her quite a bit,' said another friend. 'She's mourning, and trying to figure out what to do next. The family are showering Matilda with love right now.'

Not everybody had handled Heath's death with the due respect. The *Entertainment Tonight* TV show was ready to air, on 31 January, a video allegedly showing the actor at a 'drug-filled party' in 2006. Several stars, including Natalie Portman and Sarah Jessica Parker, successfully petitioned the show not to screen it. In *The Guardian*, Germaine Greer criticised the 'health practitioners' who had prescribed Ledger's medication. He was, she added, 'being persecuted by the unspeakable Australian press. His body, strapped flat to the gurney as the paramedics removed it from his apartment, struck me as much too thin to be that of the well-set young man I had breakfast with in Berlin two years ago.'

ABOVE: Press and fans gathering outside Heath's apartment in Manhattan after news of his death broke

ABOVE: Diane Wolozin, the masseuse who, along with Heath's housekeeper, discovered his body

She continued, 'An actor such as Ledger, who seems to tear his best work out from somewhere deep inside him, is as highly tuned and fragile as an athlete. (Yet) Ledger was left to take care of himself . . .'

Nicole Kidman and Mel Gibson had been among the first stars to pay tribute. 'What a tragedy. My heart goes out to his family,' said Kidman, with whom Ledger had come close to co-starring in Baz Luhrmann's new epic *Australia*. Instead, he had opted to do *The Dark Knight*.

Gibson, who had mentored the younger actor in *The Patriot*, said, 'I had such great hopes for him. He was just taking off, and to lose his life at such a young age is a tragic loss.'

John Travolta commented, 'He was one of my favourite actors. His abilities are rare.'

Leading Australian journalist and producer Clint Morris remarked, 'The whole of Australia is in deep shock. I liked Heath, he was a good guy.' Some wondered how Warner Brothers would react given the problems this would pose to the new *Batman* movie. In the event they were tasteful. President of Warners, Alan Horn, said, 'The entertainment community has lost an enormous talent. Heath was a brilliant actor and an exceptional person.'

In the scramble for quotes, Hollywood legend Jack Nicholson was awkwardly misrepresented. Nicholson, who of course played The Joker in Tim Burton's 1989 *Batman*

movie, was in London at the time of Heath's death. It was first reported that, asked for a reaction, he quietly replied, 'I told him so.' The media took this to imply that he'd warned Heath of the pitfalls of sleeping pills. The next day he claimed he was horrified to be misquoted. He stated that he'd never even met Ledger. 'What I actually said was, "I warned them." I had a bad experience with those sleeping pills. I took one and had just gone to sleep when I had a phone call to go to an emergency at a friend's house. I jumped up, went outside, and some time later woke up in the driveway. It might sound amusing, but I live in the mountains and it could have been worse. I didn't know Heath Ledger, but I know those pills.'

As Daniel Day Lewis received awards for his leading role in Paul Thomas Anderson's film *There Will Be Blood* at the Baftas, the Oscars and Screen Actors Guild Awards in late January and February, he made dedications to Ledger, a young actor who could have gone on to become one of the all-time screen greats. In fact, Lewis' fractured but beautiful SAG Awards acceptance speech is worth quoting at length, capturing as it does much of what appealed to fellow actors about Ledger's work:

'Thank you. I'm very, very proud of this . . . You know, for as long as I can remember, the thing that gave me a sense of wonderment, of renewal, the thing that teased me

ABOVE: Fans left candles, floral tributes, gifts and poems on the pavement outside Heath's apartment

with the question how is such a thing possible, and then dared you to go back into the arena one more time, with longing and self-doubt, jostling in the balance. It's always been the work of other actors, and there are many actors in this room tonight, including my fellow nominees who have given that sense of regeneration . . .

'Heath Ledger gave it to me. In *Monster's Ball*, that character that he created, it seemed to be almost like an unformed being, retreating from themselves, retreating from his father, from his life, even retreating from us, and yet we wanted to follow him, and yet we're scared to follow him almost. It was unique. And then, of course, in *Brokeback Mountain*, he was unique, he was perfect. And that scene in the trailer at the end of the film is as moving as anything that I think I've ever seen. And I'd like to dedicate this to Heath Ledger. So, thank you very much.'

Heath had given several tremendous performances, the best of all being Ennis Del Mar in *Brokeback Mountain*. His talent was exemplified by the scene in which Jake

Gyllenhaal's Jack Twist asks him, as he stares at the stars, 'Anything interesting up there in heaven?'

'I was just sending up a prayer of thanks,' murmurs an uncharacteristically content Ennis.

'For what?' wonders Jack.

Ennis winks and smiles, 'For you forgettin' to bring that harmonica. I'm enjoyin' the peace and quiet.'

While the phrase has become hackneyed through overuse, Ledger will surely live on in his films. In the summer of 2008 his image will be ubiquitous across the planet as the darkest twist yet on the Batman story, *The Dark Knight*, hogs the screens. And what an image that will be. Ledger's interpretation of The Joker is like nothing seen or imagined before. Coupled and contrasted with his wonderfully subtle work in *Brokeback Mountain*, its marvellous mayhem should prove to be his lasting celluloid legacy.

'We all loved him dearly,' said Todd Haynes. 'I have no doubt he would have made an astounding director.'

CHAPTER ELEVEN

The Killing Joke

'THE JOKER, so far, is definitely the most fun I've had
with any character,' Heath had said of his starring role
in Christopher Nolan's second Batman movie, *The Dark
Knight*. 'He's just out of control, with no empathy . . . he's a
sociopath, a psychotic, mass-murdering clown. And I'm just
thoroughly, thoroughly enjoying it! It's just exceeded any
expectation I had of what the experience would be like . . .'
Of course, Ledger's untimely death presented the makers
of the movie with a host of dilemmas: moral, artistic and
commercial. Set for high-profile release in July 2008, the
movie had been advertised and hyped up in advance
for the best part of a year beforehand.

LEFT: Heath attending a show during
the Mercedes-Benz fashion week in New
York in September 2007

ABOVE: Although his relationship with the press photographers may have hit an all-time low, Heath was happy to pose for photos with fans at the Sydney premiere of *Brokeback Mountain* in 2006

ABOVE: Heath at the Oscars Nominations luncheon in Los Angeles in February 2006

Prior to the tragedy, Heath's striking characterisation of the iconic villain The Joker had featured prominently in advance teasers and trailers. Perhaps more prominently than Batman (Christian Bale) himself. Posters had highlighted The Joker, played for the first time ever by a non-American, drawing a clown's smile on a mirror with lipstick, alongside the words 'Why So Serious?' As a studio insider candidly and pensively confessed to *Daily Variety*, 'The Joker character is dealing with chaos and life and death and a lot of dark themes. Now everyone is going to interpret every line out of his mouth in a different way.' A character conceived as part truly shocking rogue, part over-the-top camp cartoon baddie, was now, as Heath's last fully-completed role, going to be loaded with resonance and symbolism, justified or otherwise. It was, fairly or not, going to be read by some as an indication of Heath's own personal state of mind in his final months.

For all the genuine concern and compassion, it wasn't too long before the first news story to reveal that business was back to normal emerged. On 19 February, it was announced that – with his family's blessing – a Joker action-figure doll was going ahead as planned. Just a week after Ledger's funeral, toy manufacturers Mattel displayed their own understanding of his 'immortality', saying the toy figures would be marketed in tandem with the movie's release. 'Ledger Joker Doll To Go On Sale', stated dubious headlines. 'Two versions of the Heath joker doll will hit stores in May – one comes with a rocket launcher, the second is armed with a knife.' A spokesman for the Ledger family defended the decision. 'Heath was very proud of his work in the film and his family is aware and supportive of the plans for the movie.' Less debatably, the official Batman website showed class for weeks after Heath's death, offering simply the movie trailer plus a tasteful picture of Ledger and the dedication: 'We mourn the loss of a remarkable talent gone too soon, and the passing of an extraordinary man who will be greatly missed.'

The movie has yet to be screened at the time of writing, but the cast and basic storyline have emerged, alongside

ABOVE: Heath's father, Kim, mother, Sally, and sister, Kate, make a
statement to the press in Perth following Heath's tragic death

those Joker-dominated trailers. The follow-up to *Batman Begins*, wherein Nolan reinvented and redefined the ailing franchise, much desecrated in earlier versions by Joel Schumacher and Tim Burton, promises to be breath-taking, both visually and dramatically. Nolan, British-born but American-based, established his artistic reputation through such compelling films as *Memento* and *Insomnia*, reaffirming his talent in *The Prestige*.

The story will begin this time with Batman raising the stakes in his war on crime. With the help of Lieutenant Jim Gordon (Gary Oldman) and District Attorney Harvey Dent (Aaron Eckhart), he sets out to wreck the remaining criminal organizations that plague the streets of Gotham City. At first the partnership proves effective, but they soon find themselves threatened by a reign of chaos unleashed by a rising maverick mastermind known as . . . The Joker. The crime bosses are picked off, one by one. Has Batman/Bruce Wayne met his match in this crazed psychopath?

Prior to the release of any film as big as a Batman movie, even the first one not to have the word Batman in the title, there is much chatter and hypothesis. Rumours that Ledger's friend and *Brokeback* co-star Jake Gyllenhaal was to join the cast turned out to be unfounded. However, his sister Maggie

Gyllenhaal (*Secretary*, *Sherry Baby*) joined the cast as Rachel Dawes, replacing (from the previous movie) Katie Holmes, who cited 'scheduling conflicts'. Rachel McAdams and Emily Blunt had reportedly been in contention. The Harvey Dent role had been coveted by Hugh Jackman, Ryan Philippe, Liev Schreiber (Naomi Watt's significant other) and Josh Lucas. Bob Hoskins had said he'd love to play The Penguin, calling Nolan 'a fantastic director', but Nolan stated he had no desire to incorporate The Penguin, calling the villain made famous by Burgess Meredith 'too far-fetched'.

Yet it was The Joker about whom everybody wanted to know. Before Ledger's casting, Robin Williams, Paul Bettany and Adrien Brody had all expressed interest. Jerry Robinson, one of the original 1940s creators of The Joker, was hired as a consultant. The character was to be portrayed as close as possible to his first two appearances in the old Batman comics, plus his showing in the graphic novel *The Killing Joke*. *The Joker's Five-Way Revenge* was an influential source, too. Thus, the high camp of, in different eras, Cesar Romero and Jack Nicholson would be largely bypassed. To prepare himself, the 'fearless' Ledger lived alone in a hotel room for a month, developing The Joker's idiosyncrasies and mannerisms. He cited late Sex Pistol

and punk figurehead Sid Vicious and the character of Alex in Anthony Burgess' *A Clockwork Orange* as inspirations as well as Malcolm McDowell's interpretation of Alex in the controversial landmark Stanley Kubrick film. Ledger himself conceded he was finding the role very taxing and tiring, and was suffering acute insomnia. Nolan, with co-writers Jonathan Nolan (his brother) decided The Joker would have no 'back story' or 'origins' in the film, so as to present him as 'absolute'. The film overall would be influenced, he added, by Michael Mann's 1995 classic *Heat*, which had starred Al Pacino and Robert De Niro.

Such earnestness was not in evidence when Christian Bale was first handed the bat suit on set. As a joke, designers had fitted it with nipples. Bale was quick to cotton on and sussed instantly that it was a wind-up, but was game enough to pose for a few quick souvenir photos in the 'wrong' outfit.

In the months leading up to the film's release, complex, interactive marketing campaigns were launched online and elsewhere. At the 2007 San Diego Comic-con an event ran under the title 'Why So Serious?' This sent keen fans following clues hidden around the city. Legions of fans with

Joker face paint congregated in the street. Then, suddenly, one of them was invited into a black Escalade (with Gotham City license plates) that had just pulled up. A moment later, the fan started screaming and the SUV sped away. Later that same day, a Gotham City newspaper was circulated, reporting that a man believed to be The Joker was found beaten to death. Included were 'crime scene photos' of the fan who had been in the car. The Joker had, continued the mock report, been found with a playing card in his hand, on which was scribbled 'See you in December'. Such cryptic half-clues, sometimes deliberately misleading, only boosted fans' feverish anticipation and the heated guessing games. At Thanksgiving Weekend 2007, fake four-page *Gotham Times* tabloids were handed out at well-populated events. Articles headlined 'City at War – Batman Saves Entire Family' dropped story-line hints. The paper, naturally, reckoned the weather was 'gloomy and overcast'. There were even ads for the Gotham Girl Guides, the Gotham Bank, and the Gotham Police Dept.'s latest recruitment drive.

Actual filming in Chicago had taken place under a fake title, to throw people off the scent. *Rory's First Kiss* was the

LEFT: Michelle Williams celebrates the life of Heath Ledger at his wake at the Indiana Tea House in Cottesloe, Perth, Australia

ABOVE: Heath played The Joker opposite Christian Bale (right) as Batman in *The Dark Knight*

unlikely phoney working title taken by Nolan and team. Off-duty Chicago cops volunteered to play Gotham cops. Nolan was insistent on those 'gloomy' and 'overcast' angles. He wanted distance from the notion of Batman as a kiddies' tale, and from all the previous upbeat, multi-coloured films and TV series. There is, as yet, no Robin the Boy Wonder in his movies, for example. 'These are Batman's early days . . . Robin's out there in a crib somewhere,' Nolan has laughed. And yet, The Joker is a grim and intimidating enough creature to fit the darker tone perfectly. It was *The Killing Joke* which Nolan first handed to Ledger for reference.

Although Jack Nicholson had pioneered a scarier, more sinister Joker than commonly expected in Tim Burton's *Batman* of 1989, the cackling prankster patented by Cesar Romero in the sixties TV show tended to dominate our popular impressions. Until now. Channelling Alex and Sid, Ledger bursts across the new film's trailers with the sides of his mouth slashed, and an unnaturally wide, almost demonic, grin. Joker creators Bob Kane and Bill Finger had based their original evil-doer on Gwynplaine, 'the gypsy clown with the carved smile', a character played by Conrad

Veidt in 1928's *The Man Who Laughs*. Gwynplaine, however, had a sweet, humorous side. Ledger's Joker is a brutal murderer, the very definition of 'macabre'. If he has a sense of humour, it's a sick, twisted, remorseless one.

The Dark Knight is all about the dark side, more fascinated by its baddies than its goodies. The catalogue of villains boasts, as well as Ledger's Joker, Eric Roberts as Salvatore Maroni, Cillian Murphy returning as The Scarecrow, and Aaron Eckhart's Two-Face (after his Harvey Dent is scarred). It is rumoured Two-Face will feature more fearsomely in the third film, assuming it happens. Ledger was set to feature in the third also. There will be much re-shuffling of plot points, one presumes. Christian Bale, Michael Caine and Gary Oldman are all signed for any third film. Caine, of course, plays Bruce Wayne's loyal butler, Alfred Pennyworth.

The Joker won't be using the name Jack Napier, as taken by Nicholson in the Burton film. He will be, simply, The Joker. With that crazed laugh and smeared make-up as war-paint. A force, a presence, a whirlwind.

The filming schedule for *The Dark Knight* was also

ABOVE: Heath claimed to have had more fun playing The Joker than he had done with any other character before

ABOVE: Michael Caine returned to play Bruce Wayne's loyal butler, Alfred, in *The Dark Knight*

something of a whirlwind. It took in Hong Kong, Chicago, Los Angeles, London (including Piccadilly Circus and Battersea Power Station), Liverpool, Twickenham, Hertfordshire, Surrey and Bedfordshire.

From the trailers alone, one can glean the strain of the happily malicious dialogue The Joker delivers. 'Starting tonight,' he intones, 'people will die. I'm a man of my word'

The Gotham bank manager challenges him with, 'The criminals in this town used to believe in things. Honour. Respect. Look at you! What do you believe in?'

The Joker replies, paraphrasing Nietzsche, 'I believe whatever doesn't kill you simply makes you . . . stranger.'

To Batman, he calls out, 'You've changed things forever. There's no going back. You see, to them . . . you're just a freak! Like me!'

When Rachel knees him in the groin, The Joker guffaws, 'Ooh, a little fight in you. I like that.' Arriving on the scene,

Batman growls, 'Then you're going to love me.'

Above all, two catchphrases stand out. 'It's all part of the plan', is one. The other, already given prominence in the ads for a film that will dominate 2008, is that ambivalent, arch, ultimately haunting, 'Why so serious?'

That Heath Ledger had his serious side is beyond question. He was interested in most art forms: music, reading and writing poetry, photography, architecture. He'd spoken of wanting to try theatre work again. Yes, he regularly appeared in magazines' Sexiest Movie Stars polls the world over, but there was little he could do about that, and it suited the studios just fine. Of his acting, he said with typical honesty in 2001, 'I don't have a technique. I've never been a believer in having one set technique on how to act. There are no rules and there is no rulebook. At the end of the day, it all comes down to my instincts.

'That's the one thing that guides me through every

decision professionally. Socially, also. That's my technique. Yeah, you read through the script a hundred times. I guess I have little characteristics about myself. Sometimes, more often than not, once we start shooting I won't look at the script at all again until we finished shooting. It's kind of like it's been imprinted in my head during rehearsals. You just let it go.'

On another occasion he said, 'I feel like I'm wasting time if I repeat myself. I can't say I'm proud of my work. It's the same with everything I do: the day I say "It's good" is the day I should start doing something else.'

Perhaps he felt differently as years passed and his work markedly improved. Perhaps he anguished just too much over his performances.

'I start to get bored,' he told another interviewer. 'Not with the choices I was making, because I didn't really have a choice. The choices were being made for me . . . I was being thrown into projects. So I kind of put the brakes on that. In a sense, I destroyed my career to rebuild it again.' In that, he succeeded, graduating from the fun of *Ten Things I Hate About You* to the intense, challenging work of *Brokeback Mountain*, *Monster's Ball* and *Candy*. And to the radical inventiveness of *I'm Not There* and *The Dark Knight*. But this immersion into roles took its toll, giving the sensitive hunk his own long, dark nights of the soul.

Luck permitting, we may see Ledger in one more film after *The Dark Knight*. On the Saturday before his death he'd been in London where, clearly satisfied with the atmosphere filming *The Brothers Grimm*, he'd been shooting his second Terry Gilliam film, *The Imaginarium of Doctor Parnassus*.

Ledger was temporarily living in Islington, shooting around the Blackfriars area. The film, which looks like continuing production in due course, was to be another magical mystery fantasy. A 2009 release is still hoped for.

By then the screenplay may have been tweaked, but when Heath was involved its story was set in modern times. It accompanies Doctor Parnassus (Christopher Plummer) and his 'Imaginarium', a travelling show which offers its audiences the choice between light and joy or darkness and gloom.

It's clear what appealed to Ledger about the premise. Doctor Parnassus can orchestrate the imaginations of others. He has, however, a shady secret. He once made a pact with the Devil, trading his immortality for youth. When his first-born child, Valentina, is sixteen, he must hand her over to 'Mr Nick' (played by Tom Waits). The dreaded date approaches, but Parnassus updates the deal with Mr Nick: whoever seduces five souls first wins Valentina. Parnassus races across time and space to save his daughter, offering her hand in marriage to any man who helps him win. This being a Gilliam film, surreal landscapes and comic characters abound.

Heath Ledger was playing the character Tony. After his death, it was announced that Johnny Depp, Jude Law and Colin Farrell had agreed to help Gilliam and honour Ledger by each stepping in to play Tony in turns. Rewrites will make his appearance change as he travels between imaginary worlds.

There will, however, only ever be one Heath Ledger. 'He was,' Cate Blanchett said, 'one of the most beautiful, independent spirits of all.'